D1714719

The Year That Changed the Game

The Year That Changed the Game

The Memorable Months That Shaped Pro Football

JONATHAN RAND

POTOMAC BOOKS, INC.
WASHINGTON, D.C.

Library of Congress Cataloging-in-Publication Data

Rand, Jonathan, 1947-
  The year that changed the game : the memorable months that shaped professional football / Jonathan Rand.— 1st ed.
      p. cm.
  Includes bibliographical references and index.
  ISBN-13: 978-1-59797-215-4 (hardcover : alk. paper)
  1. Football—United States—History. I. Title.
  GV954.R38 2008
  796.332'64—dc22

                              2008008996

(alk. paper)

Printed in the United States of America on acid-free paper that meets the American National Standards Institute Z39-48 Standard.

Potomac Books, Inc.
22841 Quicksilver Drive
Dulles, Virginia 20166

First Edition

10 9 8 7 6 5 4 3 2 1

Contents

Acknowledgments

For most historians, I am sure, fifty years are just a blip on the screen. So I could not anticipate that reaching back only as far as the 1958 NFL championship game would pose a research problem. After all, I watched the Baltimore Colts' historic 23–17 overtime victory on television, and it doesn't seem so long ago. In the years before developing this project, I enjoyed wonderful interviews with several Colts and Giants players who faced off at Yankee Stadium on that momentous December day. I expected that more primary sources would be plentiful.

Even while retracing half a century, long-term memory perseveres. As the late Hall of Fame shortstop Phil Rizzuto said when I thanked him for his keen recollection of the New York Yankees' 1949 season: "Most old ballplayers can't remember what they had for lunch. But they can remember what happened fifty years ago."

Yet, as I started my research, I began to wonder, "Where did everybody go?" Lamar Hunt, founder of the American Football League, the Dallas Texans, and Kansas City Chiefs, died December 13, 2006, at age seventy-four. I enjoyed a great working relationship with him for almost three decades, but by the time I got around to writing a book chronicling some of his greatest accomplishments, he had left us—and much too soon.

Hunt was as humble and unpretentious as anyone you could ever hope to meet. Seldom was he too busy to return a phone call. He was also as unselfish an NFL owner as you could find, routinely putting the league's best interests above his own. Because of him, many other NFL owners came to share the conviction that a league was only as strong as its weakest link.

Most of pro football's other defining figures from fifty years ago have passed away, too. Pete Rozelle, Tex Schramm, Tom Landry, Sid Gillman, and Hank Stram have died since the mid-1990s. All were key players in "the year that changed the game."

Fortunately for subsequent generations, several scribes had the foresight or good timing to interview these difference makers when they were in their prime or in a reminiscing mood. Several books, therefore, became invaluable to my research. Of special help were *America's Game,* Michael MacCambridge's historical overview of the NFL; *A Proud American,* Joe Foss and Donna Wild Foss's autobiography of the first AFL commissioner; *Going Long,* Jeff Miller's oral history of the AFL; *Halas,* the autobiography of an NFL founder; *Super Tube,* Ron Powers's history of the growth of televised sports; *Tex!* Bob St. John's biography of Schramm; and *When Pride Still Mattered,* David Maraniss's biography of Vince Lombardi.

Fortunately, there are still enough giants from this era willing to share their memories and make history come alive. Special thanks to all those who graciously agreed to interviews for this book, especially Upton Bell, Raymond Berry, Bob Howsam, Sam Huff, Norma Hunt, Curtis McClinton, Bob Oates, Lee Remmel, Bart Starr, Y. A. Tittle, and Dick Vermeil. Sadly, Howsam, who seemed so sharp and full of life when I interviewed him by phone, died just a few months later, on February 19, 2008. He was eighty-nine. While no pro football history project can be adequately researched without help from the Pro Football Hall of Fame's library staff, its help was especially important for this book. With so many key figures deceased and on line materials scarce, the books, files, and microfilms preserved in Canton were especially important. My thanks also go to the Hall of Fame library staff, including Ryan Rebholz, Saleem Choudhry, Matt Waechter, and Pete Fierle.

I also am indebted to the Kansas City Chiefs' director of public relations, Bob Moore, for putting me in touch with some valuable sources. His historical research, which is reflected by the displays at the Arrowhead Pavilion, provided a wealth of information about the American Football League's formation.

This book would not have seen the light of day without the support of Kevin Cuddihy, sports editor at Potomac Books. Vicki Chamlee's diligent editing and Jen Waldrop's production work are much appreciated. My thanks go to literary agent Ed Claflin for negotiating the contract.

My wife, Barbara Shelly, never stopped encouraging me to market this project in a highly competitive environment. My teenage son, Steven, stayed away from my laptop when he knew my deadline was closing in. My older children, David and Danielle, have encouraged me in my career as an author after I retired from the sports staff of the *Kansas City Star*.

Writing a book is a lot like football. It takes a lot of people to help you succeed, and I want to thank them all.

Chronology

December 28, 1958—Alan Ameche plunges into the end zone from one yard out and gives the Baltimore Colts a 23–17 victory over the New York Giants in sudden-death overtime of the NFL championship game. The game, soon christened "The Greatest Football Game Ever Played," draws fifty million TV viewers and raises professional football to a new plane of popularity.

January 28, 1959—Giants offensive coach Vince Lombardi is hired as head coach and general manager of the Green Bay Packers, who finished 1–10–1 in 1958.

February 17, 1959—Tim Mara dies at age seventy-one. He was a legal bookmaker and sports promoter who bought the Giants for $500 in 1925 and nurtured pro football in New York.

March 1959—Lamar Hunt, having failed to buy the Chicago Cardinals from Walter and Violet Wolfner, writes a business plan for a new league while flying from Miami to Dallas.

April–June 1959—Hunt approaches potential investors for a new league: K. S. (Bud) Adams in Houston, Bob Howsam in Denver, and a group in Minneapolis.

July 28, 1959—With Hunt's permission, NFL commissioner Bert Bell reveals the formation of the AFL while testifying before a Senate subcommittee.

August 3, 1959—Hunt and Adams officially announce the new league's formation, with their franchises located in Dallas and Houston, respectively.

August 14, 1959—Six AFL owners hold the league's first organizational meeting. They agree on the league's official name and to play a schedule in 1960.

August 29, 1959—Chicago Bears owner George Halas and Pittsburgh Steelers owner Art Rooney, who head the NFL expansion committee, announce plans to expand to Dallas and Houston for the 1961 season.

October 11, 1959—Bert Bell, NFL commissioner since 1946, dies of a heart attack while watching the Philadelphia Eagles defeat the Pittsburgh Steelers at Franklin Field.

October 28, 1959—Buffalo, with Ralph Wilson as the principal owner, is granted the AFL's seventh franchise.

November 16, 1959—A Boston group, led by Billy Sullivan, receives the AFL's eighth franchise.

November 22, 1959—AFL owners, meeting in Minneapolis, hold their inaugural draft. With teams allowed to make territorial choices, the Oilers draft LSU running back Billy Cannon and the Texans draft SMU quarterback Don Meredith.

November 23, 1959—AFL owners agree to negotiate a league-wide television contract and equally share their rights fees. The league is reduced to seven teams when news breaks that Halas has persuaded the Minneapolis owners to defect to the NFL.

November 30, 1959—The NFL holds its draft, and the Los Angeles Rams draft Cannon first overall. The Rams' general manager, Pete Rozelle, secretly signs Cannon to a three-year contract.

November 30, 1959—Joe Foss is hired as the AFL's first commissioner.

December 13, 1959—The Packers defeat the San Francisco 49ers, 36–14, and finish 7–5, their first winning record since 1947. Lombardi receives the NFL Coach of Year Award.

December 27, 1959—In an anticlimactic rematch of the 1958 NFL championship game, the Colts stage a twenty-four-point surge in the fourth quarter and win 31–16. Tom Landry, coach of the Giants' defense, signs a personal services contract to coach the proposed Dallas team.

December 29, 1959—Adams signs Cannon to a personal services contract to play for the Oilers. The deal calls for $110,000 over three years plus a Cadillac for Cannon's father and half interest in a string of service stations.

January 1, 1960—The Oilers sign Cannon to an AFL contract under a goalpost at Tulane Stadium after LSU's 21–0 loss to Mississippi. This deal sets the stage for a legal battle with the Rams and a war between the leagues. LSU halfback Johnny Robinson and Mississippi fullback Charlie Flowers, who had both signed with NFL teams, also jump to the AFL after the game.

January 7, 1960—Sid Gillman, recently fired by the Rams, jump-starts a Hall of Fame career by signing a three-year contract to coach the Los Angeles Chargers.

January 26, 1960—Rozelle is elected NFL commissioner on the twenty-third ballot in Miami Beach and soon moves the league's office to New York.

January 28, 1960—Dallas is awarded an NFL franchise to start play that year. Minneapolis officially withdraws from the AFL and receives an NFL franchise for 1961.

January 30, 1960—The AFL admits Oakland as its eighth original franchise.

Introduction

Some would argue that professional football became America's premier sport through a slow, painstaking evolution starting with the 1920 formation of a fourteen-team circuit that became the National Football League. This book argues in favor of the Big Bang—an explosion on December 28, 1958, that set off subsequent explosions, which in thirteen months transformed pro football from a fringe sport to a rocket ship flying across the nation's sports horizon.

The Baltimore Colts' 23–17 victory over the New York Giants in the 1958 NFL championship game has been known ever since as "The Greatest Football Game Ever Played." That title remains unchallenged even as that game approached its fiftieth anniversary on December 28, 2008. While some might quibble over whether that was, in fact, pro football's greatest game, who would dispute its stature as pro football's most influential game? It caused a seismic shift in the sport's popularity and ushered in the year that changed the game.

Fullback Alan Ameche's famous one-yard touchdown run for the Colts in sudden-death overtime marked the sport's coming of age. Pro football, like some gangly high school kid, went into the 1958 championship game all arms and legs, yet barely a year later it was filled out and ready to take on the world. The sport grew a good foot taller and its voice got deeper. Thirteen months of percolating history saw professional football reach manhood.

The cast from the 1958 championship game reads like a who's who of all-time greats and a branch of the NFL family tree. Fifteen players or coaches involved in that game went on to earn busts in the Pro Football Hall of Fame. Several moved to other teams and bigger roles, sinking their footprints even deeper into their game's history.

For one, Vince Lombardi, coach of the Giants' offense in 1958, took over the Green Bay Packers in 1959. There he built a dynasty that captivated America. He also helped make the Super Bowl an immediate hit because Lombardi's Packers headlined the first one. Next, Tom Landry moved from the Giants' sideline to Dallas late in 1959. His move eventually led to the Cowboys growing from haplessness to greatness. Under Landry's direction Dallas became "America's Team," which led to a worldwide following for both the Cowboys and pro football.

Weeb Ewbank, who coached the Colts to back-to-back NFL championships, continued to make history as a coach in New York. He orchestrated the most famous upset in pro football history by guiding the Jets to a Super Bowl victory over the Colts in January 1969. John Unitas, Ewbank's quarterback with the Colts, gave pro football a blue-collar hero while Joe Namath, Ewbank's quarterback with the Jets, gave pro football a counterculture hero. Sam Huff, the middle linebacker for the Giants in the 1958 title game, made himself and other top defensive players famous.

The 1958 championship game's telecast reached some fifty million viewers, then the largest television audience ever for an NFL game. It inspired one viewer, Lamar Hunt, to cast his lot with professional football. Son of billionaire oilman H. L. Hunt, Lamar was a sports-crazy youngster who played football at Southern Methodist University. He planned to buy a franchise for his hometown, Dallas, but was not sure whether to pursue professional baseball or the NFL.

For Hunt, "the greatest game" was an arrow pointing to his future. First he helped form the American Football League, which later combined with the NFL for the most meaningful merger in the history of professional sports. The two leagues then created the Super Bowl, the NFL's showpiece event, which led to pro football passing Major League Baseball as the national pastime. Since the Harris Poll in 1985 began asking sports fans to identify their favorite sport, pro football has come out on top every year. It outpolled baseball by a two-to-one margin as the 2008 NFL season dawned.

Hunt understood that the 1958 championship game, and how well suited it appeared for television, hinted at a robust future for pro football. He asked NFL commissioner Bert Bell if he might acquire a team for Dallas, but Bell told him the league had no plans to expand. So Hunt formed his own league, the AFL, in August 1959. He and his partners recruited cities and players the NFL had passed over, and there were plenty of both. The older league, finally shaken from its slumber by the threat of competition, moved into new cities, too. This development ignited a grim and expensive struggle between the leagues that eventually led to a strong and unified sport.

In the short run, the NFL would learn there was hell to pay for rejecting Hunt. In the long run, pro football was reinvented. Bell's successor, Commissioner Pete Rozelle, though a reluctant partner in the merger, led pro football to the mountaintop. A half century after the war between the leagues was declared, the NFL boasted thirty-two prosperous franchises. The Cowboys, valued at $1.5 billion, were the most prosperous of all the teams.

Rozelle was shrewd, personable, persuasive, and ambitious. The NFL, however, was not terribly ambitious before the Colts and Giants clashed. The league seemed content with the status quo and had no itch to grow. It included a dozen franchises and had not expanded since 1950, when it absorbed three teams from the failed All-America Football Conference. Most NFL owners figured that allowing more teams would only mean more slices of the pie they would have to share. They would not support expansion until it seemed their best bet for nipping Hunt's league in the bud.

The NFL had shrunk significantly since the 1920s, while not straying far from the Northeast and Great Lakes region. In 1959, the league's southernmost city was Washington, D.C., and while there were franchises in Los Angeles and San Francisco, none existed between the West Coast and the Mississippi River. Parochialism was a self-constructed barrier between pro football and its vast potential. The college game was booming in many areas where pro football would not go. The NFL, like the National Basketball Association and National Hockey League, lived off a short list of franchises and a regional following.

Powerful forces, momentous events, and visionary leaders were about to change all that. Bell suffered a fatal heart attack during a game at Franklin Field in Philadelphia on October 11, 1959. The league's awakening started on his watch and might have ended there, too, had not NFL owners found a worthy successor.

They fought long and bitterly before finding one. After twenty-three ballots, they compromised and chose Rozelle. The new commissioner moved the league offices to New York, where he oversaw the NFL's marriage to television. Eventually the league would hold $20 billion in television contracts on the fiftieth anniversary of the 1958 championship game. The NFL's history cannot be written without Rozelle, nor without the events of the thirteen months preceding his election. He was no bit player during the mayhem of 1959. As the Los Angeles Rams' general manager, Rozelle had escalated the war between the leagues by signing Louisiana State halfback Billy Cannon before his college eligibility expired. This maneuver led to Cannon being courted, and signed, by the AFL's Houston Oilers, which made him the first $100,000 professional football player. This tussle initiated a vicious, expensive, seven-year signing war that ultimately led to Rozelle belatedly endorsing the merger and building a sports kingdom.

Rozelle's career kept crisscrossing that of Tex Schramm, who was hired to get the Dallas franchise up and running in 1959. He, in turn, hired Landry, who was ready to leave football. Later Schramm was instrumental in negotiating the merger with Hunt and the AFL, as he began to emerge as one of the NFL's most influential executives of the Rozelle era.

Once pro football rounded the corner of the 1950s, there was no turning back. The tone of the 1960s proved as serendipitous for football as the late 1940s and 1950s proved for baseball. The fifties were all about a lazy fly ball and the sixties a bone-rattling tackle. Happy days were gone. America became angry. America lost its innocence in the sixties, and football never had any. Its violence, passion, and pace seemed exactly what America wanted as it moved from the Eisenhower to the Kennedy administrations.

Just as the fifties were a gateway to the jarring changes of the sixties, the 1958 championship game marked the NFL's transition from a face in the crowd to leader of the parade. The sport's magical months after Ameche's touchdown had a multiplier effect. A one-yard run became a quantum leap. That one year of change produced fifty years of success, making the great game's aftermath worth a closer look.

1

The Game That Changed the Game

If the Baltimore Colts were going to come up short in the 1958 National Football League championship game, careless preparation would not be the culprit. Coach Weeb Ewbank's meticulous pregame notes reveal he was leaving little to chance except the bounce of the ball. He addressed every detail imaginable to make sure the Colts were ready to face the New York Giants in the biggest pro football game of the year and, as it turned out, of all time.

Long after his players forgot everything else Ewbank drilled into them during two weeks of preparation before their 23–17 overtime victory, they remembered his pregame speech on December 28 at Yankee Stadium. Ewbank, a stocky man with a crew cut and a bulldog face, sent his players out of the dressing room with a chip on their shoulders. The Colts were favored by three and a half points, but Ewbank took care to cast them as underdogs.

The Colts, Ewbank told them, were castoffs being denied their rightful respect. They were, he wrote in his notes, a "Team Unknown or Not Wanted." He presented an obvious contrast to the glamour and celebrity of the Giants on New York's grand stage. "Are We Known?" Ewbank continued. "This is the place to win!"

Ewbank's entire sport, in truth, was struggling for big-time recognition before Bert Rechichar kicked off for the Colts. Pro football had entered the 1950s in the shadows of big-league baseball and college football, but midway into the decade it began to raise its profile. America's sports fans sat up and took notice when the Giants overwhelmed the Chicago Bears 47–7 in the 1956 title game. Having a championship team in New York, the nation's biggest media market, proved serendipitous for the NFL because its great ally, network television, was then coming into its own as well.

The Colts' historic victory was played before 64,185 fans in Yankee Stadium, fifty million TV viewers, and a worldwide radio audience. Once fullback Alan Ameche plunged into the end zone after eight minutes and fifteen seconds of the NFL's first sudden-death overtime, pro football would never be the same. *Sports Illustrated* headlined the Colts' victory as "The Best Football Game Ever Played." In the public mind and the sport's lore, it quickly became "The Greatest."

Ewbank had rebuilt the Colts almost from scratch after owner Carroll Rosenbloom hired him in 1954 off Paul Brown's staff in Cleveland. Ewbank kept finding hidden gems—players who were out of the league, traded from other teams, or miscast in their roles. John Unitas, one of the top quarterbacks of all time, was playing semipro football in Pittsburgh for six dollars a game in 1955. Although the Steelers had drafted Unitas, Coach Walt Kiesling cut him quickly because he considered Unitas not smart enough to be his quarterback. Based on a letter of recommendation, Ewbank gave Unitas a tryout in 1956 and liked what he saw.

"Unwanted by Steelers—but we are happy with him," Ewbank noted of Unitas. In records preserved by the Pro Football Hall of Fame in Canton, Ohio, Ewbank listed players to be addressed in alphabetical order, with a comment scrawled beside each name. Unitas was listed twenty-eighth and last because Ewbank did not have time for all thirty-six. "Many others but time is pressing," he wrote.

His players, presumably, did not have to wait for Ewbank to get all the way down the list to Unitas to understand his message: they all had been sold short by other teams. A sampling of his remarks, with his spelling, grammar, and punctuation left intact, follows.

Halfback L. G. Dupre: "49ers and Giants smiled when I took him
in draft."
Halfback Lenny Moore: "They laughed at me again—said no one
could get him to play Natl. league football. He can be just as
Great as he makes up his mind to be."
Left tackle Jim Parker: "A questionable #1 choice—Where would
you play him. I hope [Giants defensive tackle Andy] Robustelli
knows where he is playing today."
Finally, the coach wrote,

Oh, yes, Ewbank. No one Knew Him Either—just them tackles
I use to work in Cleveland. Last but not least—being a poor
boy all my life. I didn't know any millionaires. I never heard of
Carroll Rosenbloom. Yes, we all have a lot to be thankful for
and a lot of showing to be done—get out there and get ready.

Ewbank's notes, on first reading, seem complimentary. But
when he spoke, he called out his players, challenging them to prove
they deserved to stand on the verge of winning a championship. His
challenge produced its intended effect. Hall of Fame defensive end Gino
Marchetti said,

In fourteen years, I heard 'em all. "Win for Mother . . . win for
Father . . . don't disappoint all those people watching on TV."
But Weeb really put it to us. He went down the roster, name
by name. "[Art] Donovan, they got rid of you—too fat and too
slow. . . . Ameche, Green Bay didn't want you. . . . [Big Daddy]
Lipscomb, you were released. . . . [Raymond] Berry, people
said you'd never be a pro." Yeah, he named me, Unitas. He
didn't miss anybody.

Berry, who made twelve catches for 178 yards and a touchdown
against the Giants, counted Ewbank's speech among just a few that were

memorable throughout his college and pro career. Berry was the Colts' twentieth-round draft choice in 1954, though he still had a year left at Southern Methodist University. He had spent so much time on the bench before his senior year, he said, that he was surprised to be drafted.

> It was kind of interesting how many guys were in the category of being released other places, not well thought of, free agents or unknowns, like Unitas and me. He was right in what he was talking about. I had no idea if it had an effect—when it came down to playing a football game, I was a one-track, focused guy. Speeches by coaches, I never really was affected by them.

Ewbank also determined it could not hurt to mention a 24–21 loss on November 9 at Yankee Stadium. "They beat us once—they can do it again," he cautioned. He reminded his players that after that game, the Giants' quarterback, Charlie Conerly, in a bylined column for a New York newspaper claimed the Colts had been "out-gutted." The column was ghostwritten, but Ewbank played it for all it was worth.

The Colts were the fresher team. They had not played for two weeks while the Giants had had to survive a hard-fought 10–0 victory over the Browns a week earlier in an Eastern Conference playoff game. "Had no contact for two weeks—will be fat and out of shape," Ewbank fretted in his notes. But the flip side was that the Giants might be worn out. "Go after them early and it will be easy all day," Ewbank instructed. "Hit them—they can't take it—easily discouraged. . . . [Colts have] best offense in the league. Still is, if we go after them."

On the one hand, the Colts, Western Conference champions, led the twelve-team league in scoring with 381 points. Unitas, Berry, and Moore—a running and receiving threat—were headed for the Hall of Fame. The Giants, on the other hand, ranked ninth in points scored, and fans sometimes booed their offense at home. Still, Ewbank took nothing for granted, and according to author and former *Baltimore Sun* columnist John Steadman, receivers coach Bob Shaw was sent to spy on the Giants. Rosenbloom encouraged the mission and assured Shaw he would find him another job should the anxious coach be caught spying and expelled from the league.

Shaw traveled to Yankee Stadium while the Giants were practicing the week of the championship game, but he couldn't find an unlocked gate. He entered a high-rise apartment building overlooking the stadium, took the elevator to the roof, and used binoculars to watch the team practice. He noted that Conerly wasn't taking many repetitions, a tip-off that he was sore. Except for a double reverse featuring halfback Frank Gifford, the Giants showed no new wrinkles. Ewbank was reassured that he need not prepare his defense for a new bag of tricks.

Both teams finished 9–3 for the regular season. The Giants yielded just 183 points, fewest in the NFL, and were considered dominant on defense. The Colts, however, ranked second with just 203 points allowed and actually gave up fewer yards than the Giants. The prospect of the Giants' defense trying to foil the Unitas-led juggernaut promised a classic matchup.

"When we started playing, they only used to introduce the offensive players," Giants middle linebacker Sam Huff recalled. "Defense was second-class citizens. This game was so tough and so good and so wonderful, I think the defense started getting recognition, and they get equal recognition now. It was a very big game for the defensive players across America."

The Colts, after a seventy-minute flight from Baltimore, arrived at LaGuardia Airport the day before the game at 11:10 A.M. New York was experiencing seasonally chilly weather and a newspaper strike, which had begun on December 11 as deliverymen shut down the city's nine major dailies and their combined circulation of 5.8 million. New York's television and radio stations thus dominated local pregame reporting and expanded their coverage to fill the newspaper void.

The Colts held an afternoon practice Saturday at Yankee Stadium and then returned to the nearby Concourse Plaza Hotel. They met for a team meal at 4:30 P.M. and went into meetings two hours later. A snack at

9:30 was followed by a bed check at 10:00. This ordinary routine preceded what would prove an extraordinary game.

Sunday dawned windy and chilly, but the sun broke through the clouds and conditions were as favorable as could be expected in late December. The Colts' charter buses left for the stadium at 12:30 P.M. for a 2:05 P.M. kickoff. Some fifteen thousand Colts fans, hoping to see Baltimore's first major sports championship in the twentieth century, crammed the bleachers.

The Giants won the coin toss and elected to receive. Rechichar, who had set an NFL record with a fifty-six-yard field goal in 1953, boomed the kickoff into the end zone for a touchback. Out came the New York offense led by backup quarterback Don Heinrich, whose accuracy for the season was merely 38 percent. Coach Jim Lee Howell sometimes wanted Conerly to study the opposing defense from the sideline while Heinrich probed its tendencies. This strategy seemed peculiar, especially when the Giants could not manage a first down on three possessions with Heinrich. He fumbled away the ball on the second drive.

But the Giants kept the Colts' offense in check, too. Huff set the tone for the Giants on the Colts' first series by blasting Unitas on a third-down blitz and forcing a fumble, which was recovered by Giants safety Jimmy Patton. The Colts' next drive ended when cornerback Lindon Crow intercepted a Unitas pass for Berry. That turnover would mark one of the few times that day the Unitas-Berry connection would be interrupted.

Berry was a precise and reliable possession receiver and Moore a game breaker. Unitas started his third possession by calling a fly pattern for Moore, who burned Crow for a sixty-yard pickup before Patton made the tackle. Though that drive ended with Huff blocking Steve Myhra's twenty-seven-yard field goal attempt, Moore's deep threat would leave the Giants' secondary bomb-shy all game. That looser coverage left plenty of room over the middle for Berry, and Unitas played by the motto "You take what they give you."

Conerly's entrance late in the first quarter brought the Giants' offense to life. The Colts, expecting a run up the middle on third and one, were fooled when Gifford broke around the left end for thirty-eight yards. That gain set up Pat Summerall's thirty-six-yard field goal for a 3–0 lead. A grim struggle was building.

Conerly opened the second quarter with a short sideline pass to Gifford, who fumbled to tackle Ray Krouse at the Giants' twenty-yard line. The Colts scored with five straight running plays. Ameche hit the right side for a two-yard touchdown run, and Myhra's kick gave the Colts a 7–3 lead.

Then the Giants, who were forced to punt on their next possession, got a huge break. Jack Simpson, who'd returned only one punt all season, fumbled Don Chandler's kick at the Baltimore ten, where Melwood Guy recovered it. But the Giants returned the favor. Gifford fumbled on a first-down sweep, and end Don Joyce recovered at the fourteen. Unitas then offered a preview of how he would pick apart a great defense. He orchestrated a fifteen-play, eighty-six-yard drive, which he kept alive with a sixteen-yard scramble. Unitas finished the drive with a fifteen-yard touchdown pass to Berry, who split the safeties, Patton and Emlen Tunnell.

The Colts led 14–3 at halftime and almost broke the game open in the third quarter. A thirty-two-yard pass from Unitas to tight end Jim Mutscheller led to a first down at the three. But the Giants' defense rose to the occasion. Ameche ran left to the one, and Unitas was stopped cold on a sneak. On third down, Ameche was stopped on a run up the middle. The Colts, rather than try a field goal, called for an option pass by Ameche. This gadget play nearly cost the Colts a championship. Mutscheller was wide open for the pass, but Ameche misunderstood the call and ran wide with a pitchout from Unitas. Linebacker Cliff Livingston threw Ameche for a four-yard loss.

Unitas recalled,

What Ameche didn't hear was the "four-hundred" series. That requires the back that gets the ball to throw the pass. All he heard was "twenty-eight," which basically was a pitchout. If you look at the film, you see Mutscheller standing back there all by himself. All he had to do was flip it over there. There wouldn't have been a need for the overtime.

That blunder slowed the Colts and inspired the Giants, who, despite their offensive lulls, had some big-play threats. On third and two from his own thirteen-yard line, Conerly found wide receiver Kyle Rote open behind the secondary. Rote caught the ball and ran to the Colts' twenty-five-yard line, where Andy Nelson ran him down and knocked the ball loose. Halfback Alex Webster, trailing the play, picked up the ball on the run and reached the one-yard line before cornerback Carl Taseff knocked him out of bounds. Fullback Mel Triplett plunged over right guard two plays later, and the Giants trailed 14–10. It was anyone's game to win now.

Conerly kept firing away. On the next drive, he found wide receiver Bob Schnelker for seventeen yards as the third quarter ended. Then he hit Schnelker for forty-six yards to the Colts' fifteen. Conerly closed out the drive with a fifteen-yard touchdown pass to Gifford. With Summerall's kick, the Giants led 17–14. All they needed was for their vaunted defense to hold the lead, and it met the challenge deep into the fourth quarter. Huff broke up a third-and-eleven pass for Moore that led to a forty-six-yard field goal try by Rechichar. The kick fell short. When a fumble by Giants halfback Phil King gave the Colts possession at the New York forty-two, Robustelli's and tackle Dick Modzelewski's back-to-back sacks of Unitas forced the Colts to punt.

The Giants took over at their nineteen-yard line and tried to run out the clock. A ten-yard pass to Webster picked up a first down at the thirty-four and two plays later the Giants faced third and four at their own forty. The Colts' linebackers dropped into coverage, which boded well for Conerly's call—a Gifford sweep around the right side, with Webster throwing a lead block and both guards pulling. Webster blocked Taseff to the outside and Gifford cut inside. Marchetti, however, shed Schnelker's block and tackled Gifford near the first-down marker. The game's major controversy ensued.

"Gino grabbed Gifford first and then [linebacker Don] Shinnick stood him up," recalled center and linebacker Dick Szymanski. Lipscomb charged in late, prompting Donovan to recall, "Lipscomb, he put about five guys on our team out of commission piling on." Lipscomb, a 288-pound tackle, fell on Marchetti and broke his ankle. Referee Ron Gibbs called time-out for Marchetti's injury and a measurement. Gifford seemed certain he had gotten the first down until head linesman Charlie Berry spotted the ball.

"Laying down on the ground, [Gifford's] screaming and hollering, 'I made that first down! I made that first down!'" Donovan recalled. "I said, 'Why don't you shut up and go back to the huddle? You didn't make it.'"

Gifford has begged to differ for decades. "I know I made it," he insisted. "But Marchetti broke his leg, and he was screaming like a wounded panther. There was a lot of confusion. A lot of time passed by while they carried Marchetti off the field. When they spotted the ball, it was placed short of the first-down marker."

The next day, however, Howell invited New York sportswriters to join him while he reviewed the game film. Joe Trimble of the *Daily News* wrote that the spot of the ball appeared correct. "Judging from the films, head linesman Charlie Berry didn't make a mistake," he wrote.

The third-down play shows Gifford reaching the New York 43-yard line, plus maybe a few inches. He didn't appear to reach the 44, which was necessary for the first down. Howell stopped the action and re-ran it a couple of times, almost in the hope Giff might get that needed distance. But each time the play ended, Frank was in the same place. The coach shook his head: "We thought he made it all right but it doesn't show there. And it happened right in front of our bench."

Howell was heavily second-guessed for punting rather than trying to pick up the first down that could have clinched a victory. With Marchetti sidelined, some reasoned, the Giants could have picked up the first down by running at his replacement. Left tackle Roosevelt Brown, who usually ripped off his helmet when it was time for the kicking unit to come on the field, kept his helmet on and jabbed his index finger toward the end zone. He clearly wanted to go for it.

"We had the league's best punter, or at least the second best," Howell explained, referring to Chandler's gross average of forty-four yards, which was second only to that of Washington's Sam Baker. "And our defense was playing well, so I decided to punt and hope that the defense would hold them. The players were upset that we didn't go for it. Even my wife thought I had made the wrong call, but I'd do it again."

Ewbank agreed with Howell and said, "The field was in bad condition and they had a strong punter, so I couldn't criticize his decision. If things were turned around, I would've punted, too."

As Marchetti, on a stretcher, insisted on watching the Colts' final drive, Chandler punted forty-three yards, and Taseff made a fair catch at the fourteen. The Colts were eighty-six yards from the New York goal line with one minute, fifty-six seconds left. "I said to myself, 'Well, we've blown this ballgame,'" Berry recalled. "The goalpost looked a million miles away."

It didn't look that way after the Colts went into a no-huddle offense. The Giants were in a prevent defense, taking away sideline routes and deep throws to Moore. Unitas's first two passes fell incomplete, but he got a first down with an eleven-yard pass to Moore at the twenty-five. A twenty-five-yard catch and run by Berry placed the ball at midfield with sixty-four seconds left. Unitas came back to Berry on the left side for fifteen, then twenty-two yards. The Colts had no timeouts left and rushed their kicking unit on the field. Myhra's twenty-yard field goal with seven seconds left tied the score 17–17.

The twenty-five-yard completion to Berry, the first of three straight completions to him in less than a minute, put the Giants on their heels.

"That was the door opener, that was the key," Berry recalled.

That goes back to the relationship John and I had been developing for three years. The reason that pass was completed was we studied together, rehearsed together about situations— "What do we do if they do this?"

This particular situation, we had probably been working on for two years. The route was a ten-yard square-in—we called it the "L" pattern. What do we do if a linebacker walks right up on us? You don't run an "L" pattern with a 250-pound linebacker breathing down your neck. So you make a quick fake, hope the linebacker tries to hit you, and try to get away from him. We called it the "linebacker slant."

We had two weeks to prepare and I'm spending a tremendous amount of time studying film and I'm not sure we ever saw them go to a defense where [Harland] Svare walked up on me. It was second-and-ten and we called two plays in the huddle because we're out of timeouts. When I walked up to the line of scrimmage, Svare is right in my face. I looked at [Unitas], he looked at me, so when the ball's snapped, he's ready. I caught it about six yards deep, faked to the outside, and when he reached to hit me, I got underneath him.

Visualize the defense now. They've just given up a twenty-five-yard gain and the offensive team is right back on the line of scrimmage with no huddle. They're scrambling to get lined up with no time to talk and we snap the ball. Nobody was using the no-huddle offense then. This was the accidental no-huddle. I think it really did affect the Giants' ability to react. You get your opponent off balance and interfere with his ability to think. That was a huge factor in being able to complete those three passes in the last two minutes. The third one was a ten-yard hook pattern and I gave an inside fake and [cornerback Carl] Karilivacz fell for it and I could run until Jimmy Patton hit me. They were all inside routes and the last one took the ball into field goal range with the clock still running.

Considering that Myhra made only four of ten field goal tries and missed three extra points during the regular season, the twenty-yard kick did not seem a given. He had missed from twenty-four yards in the first quarter and then, after an offsides penalty, saw his second chance blocked. "I told myself I better not miss it or it was going to be a long, cold winter back on the farm in North Dakota," Myhra said.

The Giants had time for one play, and Conerly ran a sneak, pushing the NFL into uncharted waters. Though the rule for sudden-death overtime in a postseason game was adopted in 1941, it had never been used. Some players, Huff included, assumed the game was over. "I was happy the score was tied and at least I got half the money," he recalled. "But the referee came to the sidelines and said it was sudden death. We'd have a kickoff and the team that scores first, wins. I said, 'What?'"

Unitas, though famously unflappable, was puzzled, too.

We never discussed anything about an overtime. When we tied the football game, we were standing around, scratching our heads, waiting for someone to make a decision on what we were going to do. I took Gino's place as captain for the overtime [to] flip the coin, get the ball if you can. That was the first time I was aware there was going to be an overtime.

Only then did Marchetti agree to leave the sideline. "I wouldn't let them take me into the clubhouse at first," he said. "This was my game, too. I watched as we drove to Myhra's field goal. But they were afraid we'd be overrun by the crowd."

Unitas lost the coin toss by calling tails, and the Giants elected to receive. Rookie Don Maynard fumbled Rechichar's kickoff at the ten, picked it up, and brought it out to the twenty. After a four-yard run by Gifford and an incomplete pass, Conerly, facing third and six, couldn't find an open receiver. He scrambled five yards. The Giants brought on Chandler, who boomed a fifty-two-yard punt. The stage was set for one of the most famous drives in NFL history—eighty yards in thirteen plays, with Ameche's plunge ending the game.

That one drive was almost a game in itself, full of memorable plays, risky decisions, and bizarre events. It seemed aborted when Modzelewski sacked Unitas, forcing a third-and-fourteen play at the Colts' thirty-seven. The Colts tried a new formation, with both ends split wide and Moore, the intended receiver, in the slot. Moore was covered, however, so Unitas went to Berry on the left sideline for twenty-one yards and a first down at the Giants' forty-two. "In that era, before the passing game had been refined into what it is now, the perfection of Unitas and Berry—and I say perfection because they were both perfectionists—was something extraordinary," Tom Landry, the Giants' defensive coordinator, said.

Next came a classic Unitas gambit. Modzelewski had already sacked him three times, and Unitas schemed to use the tackle's fierce rush against him. Unitas had repeated success on his left side of the field, where he picked on Svare and Karilivacz. Huff's job was to key on Ameche and defend passes to Moore over the middle, but Huff had become so worried about Berry that he instead dropped into coverage to support his right cornerback. "I was going to help Karilivacz and I cheated on my position to help cover Berry and darned if they didn't run Alan Ameche right up the middle," Huff recalled. "That taught me to keep your own position."

As Modzelewski barreled in, right guard Alex Sandusky and center Buzz Nutter let him through, and then left guard Art Spinney crossed over to trap him. Huff was taken out of the play by right tackle George Preas. Ameche ran twenty-three yards to the twenty, and as he was tackled, the NBC picture went blank for the vast TV audience. Fans had knocked loose a power cable that had been run through the stands.

Screens stayed dark for two and a half minutes, and according to Berry, TV viewers might have missed the finish had he carried out his blocking assignment.

"If I hadn't loafed on that play, Ameche might've scored," Berry explained.

> I was tired, I'd been running pass patterns all afternoon. And my assignment downfield was to get the safety. One of the principles I learned about downfield blocking as a wide receiver is that on the snap you must assume the running back is going to go all the way. But that play never breaks for more than two or three yards. So I decided to take a rest and this is the only time Alan ever broke that play in his career. And here I am, loafing. I don't get on Patton and he helps bring him down.

Colts broadcaster Chuck Thompson, announcing the telecast with Giants voice Chris Schenkel, was interrupted by an urgent directive. Thompson recalled,

> Suddenly, a voice in my headset was saying, "Do a radio play-by-play." Where there had been at least a dozen people all around us just seconds before, Schenkel and I found ourselves alone in the booth with just our spotter and two technicians. Everyone else had gone to rectify the problem. Words can't describe the feeling of utter frustration and helplessness. You could cut the tension in the booth with a knife.

With only the Yankee Stadium crowd watching, L. G. Dupre was stopped for no gain. Unitas threw to Berry for twelve yards to the eight-yard line, and Ameche gained one yard on the next play. The Colts called a time-out, and Unitas asked Ewbank for instructions. The coach recalled, "I said, 'Keep it on the ground. Alan's sure, he won't fumble.

Worse comes to worst, we got the field goal.' So what did that little son of a gun do?" Unitas threw, of course.

But first, there was another delay when an apparent drunk—actually an NBC employee stalling for time—ran on the field, prompting an officials' time-out while three policemen chased him down. Finally, play resumed, and the TV picture returned as Unitas put the ball between Mutscheller and the right sideline. The tight end made the catch and went out of bounds at the one. Now it was third and goal, and Unitas would pull no more surprises. "We all knew the next play was going to be a run, and that Ameche would be carrying," Huff said. "But it didn't do much good."

Unitas called "16 Power," a plunge over right tackle. Mutscheller blocked Livingston, the left linebacker, and Moore got a piece of Tunnell. As Ameche plowed forward with his head down and left shoulder out in front, he squeezed the ball in his right hand, and there wasn't a defender who could lay a hand on him.

"We got the halfback [Moore] blocking ahead of Ameche with a double team on the tackle," Unitas explained. "When I slapped the ball in Al's belly and saw him take off, I knew nobody was going to stop him. They couldn't have done it if we needed ten yards."

Early winter darkness was settling in, and a mist danced in the Yankee Stadium lights. Players cast large shadows on the hard, barren field, though not as large a shadow as this game would cast on the history of their sport. An Associated Press photograph of Ameche scoring conveys the ghost-like atmosphere often ascribed to the closing minutes. On this day, however, no extra artistic touches were needed. The game was so rich in momentum changes, big plays, and gutsy calls that postmortems have gone on indefinitely. Forty years later, Gifford still wondered why the Giants couldn't stop Unitas from hitting one throw after another on the same side.

"Well, we had Svare beat pretty much," Unitas told him. "He was kind of confused. Raymond said he could run in front of him or behind him. It was one way for us to get Sam out of the middle. Sam got so mad at Svare, he started dropping back further every time."

Gifford also wondered aloud if Landry, a crack defensive coach, made any adjustments to stop Unitas on the winning drive. "You played your same old defense," Unitas said. "You didn't do any changing one way or the other. Svare was just supposed to get back into his hook area. He was dropping back pretty deep, so instead of dragging behind him, we just ran in front of him. I was able to get the ball to Raymond twice."

Reporters asked if the Colts had won because they were the fresher team. Had the Colts' week off while the Giants faced the Browns proved decisive at the end?

Gifford said,

A lot of our guys didn't even practice up to the Baltimore game. Just to play as well as we did is very memorable for me. I do have great memories of the game. But after the game was over, I knew that without my fumbles, we would have won. I felt terrible. [Offensive coach] Vince Lombardi came up to me. He put it all in perspective for me. It's been with me ever since. He wrapped his arms around me and he said, "Frank, don't feel bad; we wouldn't have been here without you."

Though Huff eventually concluded that the Colts were the better team, he left the field steaming over the failure of a proud defense. "I was angry," he said.

I was a very competitive football player. This was a championship game. I was making nine thousand dollars a year and I needed the money. The difference between winning and losing was a couple of grand. I just was angry the way John was able to throw that ball against us to Berry. He was certainly the difference in the football game. He knew where to attack the defense, he found the weakness. He exploited it to perfection.

I mean, if you look at the play-by-play, Unitas to Berry . . . Unitas to Berry. That still rings in my ear. We couldn't stop it. We didn't stop it. And that was the difference in the game.

Huff also concluded that playing loose on Berry was the Giants' fatal mistake. "He had a short leg, and he couldn't see. He could catch the ball—that's all he could do," Huff said, referring to Berry both having one leg slightly shorter than the other and wearing contact lenses. "We laid off of him too much. We never played bump and run."

The winners were second-guessed, too. Reporters asked Unitas why he would risk an interception on second down at the seven-yard line with the Colts needing only a short field goal to win. "When you know what you are doing, you are not intercepted," Unitas replied. "The Giants were jammed up at the line and not expecting a pass. If Jim had been covered, I'd have thrown the pass out of bounds. It's just that I would rather win a game like this by a touchdown than a field goal."

Some suggested sinister motives. Rosenbloom was rumored to have made a big bet on the game, and it was pointed out to Ewbank that a touchdown was needed to cover the point spread. "A lot of people accused me of playing the point spread," the coach said. "I didn't even know what it was."

Donovan dismissed all the what-ifs as so much hot air. "These guys, the Giants, are talking about . . . it was so close," he said. "We had 200 yards more offense than they did. They had only ten first downs. How the hell can it be that close a game? We started screwing around, you hear me? Should have been 21–3."

The Colts totaled 460 yards and twenty-seven first downs while the Giants totaled 266 yards and ten first downs. The numbers were lopsided, yet the game was a masterpiece.

NFL commissioner Bert Bell, sensing a quantum leap for the league he'd led since 1946, yelled from his box, "This is the greatest day in the history of professional football!" Bell was seen with tears in his eyes. Even the Giants' founder, Tim Mara, a legal bookmaker who had bought the Giants for $500 in 1925, was rejuvenated by the game. As season ticket orders came flooding in early in 1959, Mara was at the office every morning at seven, happily predicting, "We're gonna sell out next year." But he died February 17, 1959, at age seventy-one, cutting another one of the NFL's ties to its formative years. He had seen pro football make a huge leap when the Giants drew nearly eighty thousand to the Polo Grounds in 1925 to see Red Grange and the Chicago Bears and an even bigger leap in the 1958 game against the Colts. "He died on a real high," said Wellington Mara, who, with his brother, Jack, inherited the team.

The players, however, had not been involved in pro football long enough to appreciate the place they would all take in the sport's history. "It was a championship game, something that we were certainly happy to be able to win, regardless of how we did it," Unitas said. "But I don't think you realize it till after the fact, till all the newspaper people started getting involved."

The New York newspaper strike ended the morning after the game, but it was a magazine writer who became most famously "involved" with the game's aftermath. Tex Maule covered the game for *Sports Illustrated* and lobbied his editors to call it the "greatest" football game ever played, but for the headline of his story, dated January 5, 1959, they settled for the "best." "Pro football just wasn't Madison Avenue in those days," Maule recalled.

The sport wasn't rolling in dough, either. Shares were $4,718 for the Colts and $3,111 for the Giants. So it was no small thing when Unitas was offered $700 and Ameche $500 to appear live on *The Ed Sullivan Show*, the Sunday night of the game. Sullivan, a popular TV host, was best known for bringing on Elvis Presley and six years later would introduce the Beatles to a U.S. viewing audience.

Ameche went on the show while Unitas joined his teammates on the United Airlines' charter flight to Baltimore Friendship Airport. Unitas may have wished he'd stayed with Ameche when about thirty thousand overjoyed fans surged out of the terminal to greet their heroes. Fans jumped on the roof of a police car escorting one of the Colts' two buses and wrecked it. Fans celebrated on top of the team bus, too, before police restored order and the bus sped away.

As Huff said,

> It was the small-town Baltimore Colts, who nobody knew about, coming into the big city—the media capital of the world. If we would've won the game, it wouldn't have gone down as "The Greatest Game Ever Played." But because it was Baltimore, because it was overtime, because it was John Unitas . . . they took on the mighty Giants and beat them. If we beat them, it would've been just another championship game. It all broke just right for that to be known as "The Greatest Game Ever Played."

The view from the Colts was, predictably, different. Marchetti reflected,

> That game made such a tremendous difference. After that game, there was tremendous enthusiasm for the sport. Fans were everywhere. Stadiums filled up. And in Baltimore, I was able to open my first restaurant. It also made it possible for the guys on our team to go out and find jobs in the off-season. Winning that game, it was such a great feeling. The game became so popular, and we became prosperous.

Unitas saw the NFL enjoy phenomenal growth as he played another fifteen years and even more so after he retired. In 1998, he said, "I think that particular game accelerated football into what it's become now, for the fact that it was the most viewed game that had ever been because of the advent of TV. We were now in everybody's living rooms on just about every Sunday."

Had Unitas been stopped late in regulation or in overtime, Conerly might have joined him in Canton. Conerly said in 1988,

> The fact that we lost that game has had a big effect on me. First, if the game hadn't gone into overtime, I would have received an automobile, which was a big deal at that time. Our publicity man told me three or four minutes before the end of the game that I had won the car [for being MVP]. When they voted again, Unitas won. Also, I think if we'd won that game, I'd be in the Hall of Fame now. It would have helped my credentials. It hasn't broken my heart that I'm not in the Hall of Fame, but that was a game a lot of people were watching.

Gifford is among the 1958 Giants elected to the Hall of Fame. He became a broadcaster after the 1964 season and in 1971 started a twenty-seven-year run on ABC's *Monday Night Football*. Recalled Gifford, who joined the Giants in 1952,

> I played before nine thousand people at the Polo Grounds and when I left, you couldn't buy a Giants ticket. The fifties through the mid-sixties was the biggest growth the NFL ever had. Pro football caught on in fifty-six, when we beat the Bears, and escalated to where we were getting sixty-two thousand . . . sixty-three thousand in Yankee Stadium, and it only seated fifty-nine thousand. That's how much standing room we had there. The fire department was raising hell. But there was that kind of focus all of a sudden on pro football.

That focus became even sharper on December 28, 1958. "It had a lot of drama to it," Gifford said. "If you look at the guys that went on to the Hall of Fame, there's no question that it had maybe the best personnel that had ever been accumulated on the football field at the same time. Just incredible names."

Hall of Fame players from that game include the Colts' Berry, Donovan, Marchetti, Moore, Parker, and Unitas. Joining them from the Giants are Brown, Gifford, Huff, Maynard, Robustelli, and Tunnell. Among the coaches, Ewbank, Landry, and Lombardi are enshrined, too. "I'm sure there have been many more games just as exciting," Landry said, "but there were some other forces at work for that game. The way everything blended together—the television, where the game was played, and the fact that pro football was ripe for expansion—was the key. I consider it to be the greatest game because of its impact."

The game did not impact every New Yorker, however. Donovan grew up in the Bronx, not far from Yankee Stadium, and expected a hero's welcome in the old neighborhood when he visited after the Colts' victory. "I was there in front of Mister Goldberg's candy store where I hung out since I was six years old," Donovan recalled. "He comes out and looks at me and he says, 'Arty, you big bum, are you out of work again?' He didn't even know I played football."

Mr. Goldberg might have been the last person in New York oblivious to the sport's defining day. "That game made pro football and gave everyone who played in it an everlasting legacy," Schenkel said. "Before that game, people would ask me, 'What do you do?' And I'd say, 'I broadcast Giants games.' And they'd say, 'Oh, baseball.' It would make me mad. But after that game, that never happened again."

2

Lombardi

For Vince Lombardi, losing was the end of the world. Yet, when he walked off the Yankee Stadium field a loser on December 28, 1958, a new world was about to open up for him. For Lombardi, a native New Yorker, that world, surprisingly, was small and snowbound Green Bay, Wisconsin. If Green Bay was not the end of the world, the Packers were at the end of their rope and needed the New York Giants' brilliant but temperamental offensive coach to rescue them from more than a decade of sustained failure and, perhaps, from extinction.

The Packers' improbable survival and success story has been a source of joy to the state of Wisconsin and all of America's cheeseheads. The Packers consistently rank among the NFL's four most popular teams and, according to the Harris Poll, were tops in popularity each year from 2002 through 2005. Despite playing in a city that claimed a population of just 102,313 in the latest census, the Packers stand among the nation's sports treasures and their home stadium, Lambeau Field, among its shrines. The Packers also are the NFL's only publicly held franchise, with 4.75 million shares owned by 112,015 shareholders.

The Packers' history is filled with sharp peaks and valleys, and their valley was deep before Lombardi pulled them out. He was hired as the coach and general manager on January 28, 1959. His arrival marked an end to the inept coaching and dysfunctional management that had kept the franchise in football hell for eleven years. Some owners had told NFL commissioner Bert Bell to straighten out the Green Bay franchise or get rid of it. The romance of the little city in the big leagues was wearing thin, and it was hard to see where the Packers fit in the NFL's future. Before Lombardi arrived, they had the league's worst record, lowest payroll, and least television revenue. Why not just give the Packers a decent burial?

Former Packers public relations director and team historian Lee Remmel said,

> I think there was a very real danger. From owners around the league, there was a feeling that Green Bay's time was past. There were people of that persuasion and I remember being very concerned about the Packers leaving Green Bay because of the way the team was going, financially and artistically. But when push came to shove, Packer fans would not permit the franchise to leave.

No other coach in modern NFL history has made as immediate an impact on a franchise as Lombardi made on the Packers. In three seasons, he turned a city with a population of 62,888 in 1959 into Title Town. After finishing his apprenticeship as coach of the New York Giants' offense in the 1958 NFL championship game, Lombardi won five NFL titles and two Super Bowl games in nine seasons. The Super Bowl was quickly accepted as a mega-event largely because its first two games featured Lombardi's Packers against the American Football League's champions. For the earliest Super Bowls, the Packers' mystique was magic dust.

Few other teams played in both the NFL's Stone Age and its Super Bowl era. The Packers were founded August 11, 1919, by Curly Lambeau, who played briefly under Knute Rockne at Notre Dame, and by *Green Bay Press-Gazette* sports editor George Calhoun. The newspaper's newsroom was the site of the team's first recruiting meeting. Lambeau was the Packers' star halfback and captain and coached them for thirty-one years. Calhoun served nearly that long as the team's manager, publicist, traveling secretary, and fund-raiser. Admission to the early games was free, and Calhoun raised money by passing the hat.

Lambeau and Calhoun convinced the local Indian Packing Company, where Lambeau worked as a shipping clerk for $250 a month, to provide a practice field and jerseys bearing the company's name. The team dominated opponents in Wisconsin and surrounding states for two years and was ready for tougher competition. The company was sold to Acme Packing, and Acme executive John Clair acquired a franchise for the Packers in the American Professional Football Association in 1921. Formed a year earlier in Canton, Ohio, the league played its first official season in 1921 and changed its name to the National Football League in 1922.

The early NFL usually fielded about twenty teams and included such Midwestern cities as Canton; Akron; Rock Island, Illinois; and Muncie, Indiana. These small markets either could not keep pace with pro football's growth or were buried by the Great Depression. Of all the small cities that got in on the ground floor, only Green Bay remains in the NFL. The franchise, figuratively speaking, almost always seemed behind on the rent.

Clair was forced to withdraw the Packers from the league in early 1922 because they were caught using two Notre Dame players in a non-league game against the Chicago Supremes. The Packers were reinstated, however, when Lambeau apologized, promised to obey league rules, and paid $250, including $50 of his own money, to buy back the franchise. He named himself owner, but his first year running the Packers easily could have been their last.

Because visiting teams received guarantees, poor attendance could drive the home team into debt. The Packers bought rain insurance for a game against Racine on October 8, 1922, and a storm indeed ruined the gate. But the rainfall measured one-hundredth of an inch below the policy's requirement, and the insurance company refused to pay. The Packers were in a hole. That hole became deeper when another game-day storm struck, but *Press-Gazette* executive A. B. Turnbull advanced Lambeau the cash to cover the visitors' guarantee. Turnbull also recruited a group of local businessmen, known as "The Hungry Five," to form a nonprofit corporation for the team in 1923. A $5-per-share stock issue raised $5,000 and each stock purchaser also had to buy six season tickets. This drive marked the first of several such issues to rescue the Packers.

By 1929, the Packers had enough cash to permit Lambeau to sign top players, and the Packers won three straight NFL championships. Their rosters from 1929 to 1931 included five Hall of Famers: linemen Cal Hubbard and Mike Michalske, halfbacks Lambeau and Johnny (Blood) McNally, and quarterback Arnie Herber. The Packers finished 10–3–1 in 1932 but were only one of eight teams still standing in the face of the Depression. And by then the Packers were barely standing. They almost went under in 1934 because they owed $5,000 to a fan who had fallen out of the bleachers and sued. The Packers had bought liability insurance, but their company failed. They were saved by Henry Graass, a Circuit Court judge and a Packers fan. He ordered the team into receivership, enabling it to be reorganized in 1935 as Green Bay Packers, Inc. A stock issue raised $15,000, enough for the team to pay its debts.

That same year, the Packers signed Don Hutson, a Hall of Fame receiver who led the Packers to NFL titles in 1936, 1939, and 1944. He retired after the 1945 season, and the Packers hit the skids. They lacked the cash to compete for players with the All-America Football Conference, which signed the Packers' top draft choices in 1946 and 1947. The Packers became so strapped for cash that on Thanksgiving Day 1949 they held an old-timers' game and intra-squad scrimmage to raise cash. They again reorganized. Stock was sold for $25 a share to 1,698 shareholders.

The Packers were poor on the field, too, and Lambeau ended an era when he resigned after a 2–10 finish in 1949. Because of its corporate structure, which was run by forty-five directors and a thirteen-man executive committee, the franchise was deprived of a sense of direction. By the end of 1958, the Packers had gone through four coaches in eleven years and compiled a 37–93–2 record. Ray (Scooter) McLean finished 1–10–1 in 1958, and legendary sportswriter Red Smith, who grew up in Green Bay, immortalized McLean's record: "The Packers underwhelmed ten opponents, overwhelmed one, and whelmed one."

McLean was overmatched in his lone season by rival teams, meddlesome directors, and mischievous athletes. "When Lombardi came in there, you immediately recognized that what we were lacking was leadership," said Hall of Fame quarterback Bart Starr, who joined the Packers in 1956. "Scooter McLean would sit down and play cards with some of the players the night before a game. It was the kind of atmosphere that was very unproductive for everybody."

Players took advantage of McLean's loose ship, especially end Max McGee and running back Paul Hornung, both notorious night owls. After a 24–10 loss to the Bears, they persuaded McLean to let them stay overnight in Chicago instead of taking the train home with their teammates. McLean agreed and warned them that he did not want to read about their escapades in the Chicago newspapers. But, of course, he did.

"So Hornung and I go down and see Don Rickles at the Playboy Club and he sees us and takes a shot at us in front of everybody," McGee said. "And then we go to Chez Paree and end up with a couple of those dancing girls, and we got back to Green Bay just in time for Tuesday morning practice." McLean called both players into his office and showed them Irv Kupcinet's *Chicago Tribune* gossip column, which reported their good time in Chicago. "And he tried to put his foot down—'Never again,'" McGee recalled. "When he said he was fining us, it pained him more than it pained us. It was hard for Scooter to get tough."

It was no secret in Green Bay that the Packers' problems went far beyond the coaching. Directors often second-guessed McLean, who was obliged to speak before them every Monday and answer questions. The executive committee functioned as a front office, and the general manager did not make any football decisions. Fans' anger peaked December 9, 1958, when the team's president Dominic Olejniczak was hung in effigy from a lamppost outside the Packers' ticket office. Even management had to agree its approach was not working.

A week later, Olejniczak announced the executive committee would be reduced to seven members and its duties curtailed. He promised that the Packers would hire a general manager with a "dominant personality." McLean resigned December 17, which left the search committee to find both a coach and a general manager. Lambeau visited from his California home and campaigned for the general manager's spot, but his star had long since faded in Green Bay.

Personnel director Jack Vainisi, who stuck out like a sore thumb in the organization because of his competence, first placed Lombardi on the Packers' radar. He scouted and acquired future Hall of Fame players Starr, Hornung, linebacker Ray Nitschke, and tackle Forrest Gregg. Vainisi was the first Packers official to contact Lombardi, according to biographer David Maraniss.

"I don't have the authority to make this call, but I'm curious to know whether you're interested," Vainisi said. Lombardi was itching to become a head coach and had become depressed in the off-season when teams did not call. But it was only a matter of time before he would get his chance. He and Tom Landry, who ran the Giants' defense, were both star assistants ready to move up.

Lombardi was offered the Philadelphia Eagles' job after the 1957 season and was about to accept. Then he consulted with Giants co-owner Wellington Mara, who advised Lombardi to reject the contract because it was not guaranteed beyond one or two years and he would not be his own general manager. Lombardi stayed with the Giants, which proved a wise career choice, though Buck Shaw rebuilt the lowly Eagles into NFL champions in just three years. They would win the 1960 title with a 17–13 victory over Lombardi's Packers in Philadelphia.

By returning to the Giants in 1958, Lombardi put himself in line for head coaching possibilities at West Point and Green Bay. He would have loved to replace Earl Blaik, for whom he had worked five seasons at West Point, but the academy traditionally picked its own graduates and hired Blaik's assistant Dale Hall. Lombardi was notified he was out of the Army picture while visiting the home of the Giants' team doctor Anthony Pisani. "Do you mind if I call Green Bay?" he asked.

Vainisi had checked Lombardi's credentials with Cleveland Browns coach Paul Brown, Chicago Bears coach George Halas, NFL commissioner Bert Bell, and Blaik. All gave glowing recommendations. Vainisi, careful not to overstep his authority, suggested that Olejniczak also contact those same four experts. Lombardi was not an easy sell because he had never been a head coach above the high school level. Other candidates the Packers considered had bigger names. Iowa coach Forest Evashevski had just won the Rose Bowl. Otto Graham had ruled the NFL as the Browns' quarterback, and Kentucky coach Blanton Collier was Paul Brown's former assistant. Jim Trimble, a former Eagles and Canadian Football League coach, was in the running, too. "Who the hell is Vince Lombardi?" a local sportscaster asked when the Packers made their decision.

Mara would have liked Lombardi to replace Giants head coach Jim Lee Howell, who was poised to retire any year. Thus Mara asked the Packers to interview Landry instead. The Giants' owner claimed he released Lombardi from his contract only when the Packers agreed to let him go if the Giants' head coaching job came open. The Packers flew Lombardi to Green Bay on January 26 for an interview at the H. C. Prange Department Store, which was run by a Packers director. Former Packers star Tony Canadeo and Packers vice president Dick Bourguignon met Lombardi at the Green Bay Airport. Lombardi, a graduate of Fordham University in New York, learned that all three had graduated from Jesuit universities. He said, grinning, "Between the three of us Jesuits here, we could kick the shit out of these non-Catholics."

Vainisi urged Lombardi to demand the dual role of coach and general manager so he would have authority over personnel decisions and be able to neutralize the board's meddling. It seemed a presumptuous demand for someone who had never been a head coach or general manager. The Packers' executives appreciated the need for a strong hand, however, and offered Lombardi both positions with a five-year contract at $36,000 a year. Lombardi was back in New York when his hiring was announced January 28, 1959. "I am looking forward to the challenge," he said. "I know the Packers have a nucleus of good veteran players. I intend to build around this nucleus."

Lombardi and Green Bay seemed an odd couple. He had spent his childhood and football career entirely in and around New York City. His rough edges and accent were purely New York. His wife, Marie, was so upset by the prospect of leaving their New Jersey home for Green Bay that she asked Mara to force Lombardi to honor his Giants contract. "Marie," Mara told her, "I think Green Bay is the place for him."

Lombardi boasted, tongue in cheek, that he expected success. "After all, I need to win only two games and Green Bay will have improved one-hundred percent," he told friends. Friends at a farewell gathering gave him earmuffs and long underwear for Green Bay winters. Lombardi, actually, would need iron underwear in Green Bay because changing a losing attitude was his first order of business. The community had grown cynical, and his locker room was demoralized. "Our number one problem here is to defeat defeatism," he said.

Remmel, then a *Press-Gazette* reporter, recalled Lombardi being asked at his first news conference what kind of team he expected to field. "He said, 'You'll be proud of this football team because I will be proud of it,'" Remmel said. "He said it with such conviction, I guess I shouldn't have been surprised at the impact he subsequently had on the team and the NFL."

Lombardi rolled up his sleeves and showed the famed work ethic he demanded of players and of himself. On February 3, his first full day running the Packers, he hired coaches Phil Bengtson for the defense and Red Cochran for the offensive backfield. That same day, he also rented a house, reappointed the front office staff, ordered the remodeling of the team's offices, addressed the board of directors, held a news conference, and sat in on several meetings. He made it clear there would be no more meddling with the football team.

"I want it understood that I'm in complete command," he told the directors. "I expect full cooperation from you people, and you will get full cooperation from me in return. You have my confidence, and I want yours." He added, in a news conference, "I've never been associated with a loser and I don't expect to be now."

Lombardi put his stamp everywhere on the franchise. Bengtson wrote in *Packer Dynasty*:

> He decided how many stripes of what width and color he wanted on the jerseys. He told the janitor where to move the water cooler, and gave instructions for the nameplate on his door to read "Mr. Lombardi," not "Coach Lombardi." To the first veteran [center Jim Ringo] who came in asking to be traded to a winning team, he retorted, "*This* is going to be a winning team." If it smacked of dictatorship, that was what was needed.

Many of these changes were merely cosmetic. Building a winner would depend on the talent of his front office, coaching staff, and players. Lombardi completed his staff with offensive line coach Bill Austin, defensive backfield coach Norb Hecker, and receivers coach Tom Fears. Lombardi, who was forty-five years old, targeted young assistants who coached or played professionally. The staff's average age was thirty-eight, and he quickly put the men to work.

As soon as Cochran and Bengtson arrived, Lombardi showed them nearly five hours of film of their returning veterans. Lombardi was not impressed by what he saw. Bengtson recalled,

> Vince put it to me this way when I approached him about shoring up our pass defense: "Look, we're not just going to start with a clean slate; we're going to throw the old slate away.

If you look at the roster of returning veterans and don't see what you must have to do the job, tell me what you need. You want to move a man from corner to safety, do it. You want to take five of my offensive men and put them in the defense, give me a list of the names. You want to buy the entire Chicago Bears' line, I'll call [George] Halas and see what I can do. That's the way we've gotta go at this. We can't do it with patch jobs and prayers."

Lombardi presented a textbook case of how to rejuvenate a franchise. He and Vainisi formed a strong front office, and he recruited a talented and tireless coaching staff. And, most important, he coaxed untapped talent from his players, partly by convincing them that the Packers were on the upswing. Before Lombardi arrived, NFL coaches would threaten disgruntled players with trades to Green Bay. When the Browns traded tackle John Sandusky to the Packers in 1956, rookie tackle Bob Skoronski had greeted him, "John, welcome to the end of the earth."

Lombardi's dictatorial approach caught most Packers off guard at training camp in 1959, though a few had an inkling of what to expect. Gregg, entering the second season of a legendary career, recalled,

I didn't know anything about him, but I thought Tiny Goss, who had played middle guard on defense when I was at SMU, might. So I asked him when I ran into him at some SMU deal. Tiny never swore. But when I asked him about Lombardi, he said, "He's a real bastard."

Don (Tiny) Goss had been with the Giants only briefly but still long enough to get acquainted with Lombardi. Many Packer veterans rolling into training camp at St. Norbert College in De Pere, a ten-minute drive from Lambeau Field, would soon learn what Goss meant. McGee and fullback Howard Ferguson arrived a few days before the veterans were scheduled to report in late July. They grabbed a free supper with the rookies, who already were practicing, and then spent the night out on the town. They planned to follow this pleasant routine for the next few days.

But when they dropped in for breakfast the next morning, Lombardi brought them to his office. He told them that as soon as they ate a meal at camp, they were officially on board and would have to start practicing and obeying team rules, including curfew. Ferguson argued that they should not have to start practice yet. "Listen, mister, you get your ass out there on the field—or you get your ass out of here!" Lombardi screamed. McGee watched as the two men kept screaming. "You meet a guy for the first time and he starts chewing your ass out," McGee recalled. "I was thinking maybe I ought to go somewhere else." Ferguson never played for Lombardi.

Gregg and defensive back John Symank also planned to arrive in camp a few days early and stopped for the night in Milwaukee. Symank wanted an update on Lombardi's camp and phoned defensive tackle Dave (Hog) Hanner, a veteran who reported early. Hanner said he had been hospitalized for dehydration. Lombardi was from the old school and believed withholding water during practice both made players more disciplined and prevented stomach cramps. Gregg said,

> John and I decided we better get ourselves on up there, so we checked out of the hotel and headed for Green Bay. We got up there fairly late and we told the young boy who was in charge of the dorm that we would probably skip the morning practice and sleep in. At seven A.M., the boy is beating the door and saying that breakfast was being served and that Coach Lombardi wanted to see us when we got there.

Gregg recalls Lombardi as seeming pleasant when he and Symank introduced themselves. Then they got a rude awakening. "We did some calisthenics and figured that would be it for the morning, but then

Lombardi put us through his famous grass drills," Gregg said. "It didn't take long before I had my tongue hanging out and was worn out and I wasn't even in pads!"

Grass drills were a Lombardi favorite. Players ran in place, lifting their knees, until Lombardi ordered them to drop on their stomachs. They would bounce up, run in place, and drop again. Players soon became exhausted. Lombardi also liked the "nutcracker" drill in which a blocker tried to lead a running back past a defensive player in a confined space. The defender was supposed to shed the block and tackle the runner. Ferocious hitting ensued.

Nitschke, a vicious hitter who joined the Packers in 1958, loved contact drills. Maraniss recounted tight end Gary Knafelc's dread of practicing the power sweep against Nitschke. "He loved it," Maraniss wrote. "Blood spurting out from his knuckles, smeared on his pants, some of it his, some Knafelc's." The drill was repeated until Knafelc, who by now feared the linebacker more than he feared Lombardi, said, "Coach, by this time even Ray knows it's a sweep."

This training was not mindless violence but part of a carefully scripted routine. Lombardi's practices lasted only about ninety minutes but were incredibly intense. He simplified his playbook and made sure every player understood the reason for each assignment. When teaching blocking and tackling techniques, the coach was a perfectionist.

Biographers have reconstructed Lombardi's speech to his veterans July 23, the eve of their first practice.

> With every fiber of my body, I've got to make you the best football player that I can make you. And I'll try. And I'll try. And if I don't succeed the first day, I'll try again. And I'll try again. And you've got to give everything that is in you. You've got to keep yourself in prime condition, because fatigue makes cowards of us all. . . . We are going to win some games. Do you know why? Because you are going to have confidence in me and my system. By being alert you are going to make fewer

mistakes than your opponents. By working harder you are going to out-execute, out-block, out-tackle every team that comes your way.

I've never been a losing coach, and I don't intend to start here. There is nobody big enough to think he's got the team made or can do what he wants. Trains and planes are going in and coming out of Green Bay every day, and he'll be on one of them. I won't. I'm going to find thirty-six men who have the pride to make any sacrifice to win. There are such men. If they're not here, I'll get them. If you are not one, if you don't want to play, you might as well leave right now.

Lombardi subsequently admitted he hoped no players would walk out, and none did. Though few warmed up to him, most could appreciate what he was trying to accomplish. Gregg said,

I think the thing that sold me on Lombardi was something I saw pretty early in training camp. Under the previous coach, the linemen and linebackers got most of the heat. They pretty much left the quarterbacks, running backs and receivers alone. But one day I heard some screaming and when I looked over, here was Lombardi, walking right behind Max McGee and barking at him. The more Lombardi barked, the faster Max moved. And I thought, "Hell, this is all right. I don't mind getting my ass chewed if everybody else is going to get theirs chewed, too."

Players were not the only ones to experience Lombardi's wrath. Remmel, a *Press-Gazette* reporter during the Lombardi years, said,

I found him difficult to get close to—I don't know if I tried that hard. It was not a simple thing. I can't say he didn't have a human side because he did. He was kind to me a couple of

times. He apologized to me one time. I was covering training
camp and the offense was his baby. That particular practice,
he was moving the two-minute offense and there were
interceptions on consecutive plays. I was just making a note
of that and he shouted at me—there were fifteen hundred
fans around—"Keep that crap out of the paper—be original!"
I waited around and told him off afterwards. I said I deeply
resented his implication that I wasn't original. I figured I'd
ruptured any kind of relationship I had with him.

Most pro football reporters traveled on the teams' charter flights in
those days, and Remmel said he doubted Lombardi would let him on the
plane to Dallas for a preseason game two days after their spat. Lombardi
did not confront him on the plane, however, and, surprisingly, allowed
reporters in the locker room before the game. "At one point," Remmel
recalled, "he walked toward me and whispered, 'I'm sorry what I said
about you not being original.'"

Though Lombardi is credited with popularizing option blocking in
the NFL, he was not especially innovative. "He was incredibly persistent
and consistent," Remmel said. Lombardi executed bedrock football as
well as any other coach in history. He also proved an exceptional judge
of talent, an often-overlooked key to his success. He had a keen eye for
placing miscast players in their logical roles.

When Lombardi was hired to coach the Giants' offense in 1954, he
recognized that Frank Gifford was being spread much too thin. Gifford
was the Giants' first-round draft choice in 1952, and Coach Steve Owen
played him in both the offensive and defensive backfields and on special
teams. Exhausted and frustrated, Gifford considered quitting. Lombardi
studied films of Gifford in the off-season and realized he'd perform best
as a full-time halfback. "He came in and took me off defense and three
years later I'm the MVP in the NFL," Gifford recalled.

What would be the odds of another miscast running back with
Hall of Fame potential falling into Lombardi's lap? Yet, in Green Bay,

Lombardi inherited Hornung, the 1956 Heisman Trophy winner from Notre Dame and first overall pick of the 1957 draft. Under Lisle Blackbourn and McLean, Hornung was tried at quarterback, fullback, and halfback. "I was in such a daze," he said. "I just wanted to get out of Green Bay."

The parallels between Hornung and Gifford were striking. Both were golden boys with movie-star looks. Hornung also had a well-deserved reputation as a ladies' man, which made him a staple of Green Bay gossip. Critics were quick to blame his carefree lifestyle for his underachieving play, and they no doubt had a point. Hornung did not become a choirboy under Lombardi, but he did find focus.

Hornung wrote in *Lombardi and Me,*

> Vince changed my life, and he came along at just the right time. My first two years with the Packers were so unhappy and unsatisfying that I was ready to quit and do something else. I needed a sense of purpose and direction in my life to keep me from drifting, and that's exactly what Lombardi gave me. He told me right away that I was going to be his left halfback, just as Gifford had been in New York. No more would I have to keep switching positions. And he told me that if I didn't make it playing left halfback for him, I would not make it in pro football. Simple as that. That challenge motivated me and gave me the focus I needed. From then on, I was committed to being the best professional football player I could be.

Lombardi also installed an offense that played to Hornung's strengths. A guard who gained notice as one of Fordham's "Seven Blocks of Granite" during the 1930s, Lombardi had a special feel for the running game. Yet when he broke into the NFL, he found most coaches preferred to pass. They considered pro defenses too big and mobile to run against. Lombardi wrote,

What I think they really liked about the throwing game, was that only two or three key men had to be coordinated on the pass play, but on the running play it required split-second timing of at least seven or eight people. What it comes down to is, that to have a good running game you have to run as a coach. You have to derive more creative satisfaction from the planning and the polishing of all eleven men rather than just three or four.

Lombardi did not require his backs to always hit a predetermined hole. He wanted them to read their blocks and spot the hole as the play developed. Nor did he require his linemen to open a particular hole. As long as daylight opened somewhere, that was fine with Lombardi. He explained,

When I first got to Green Bay, I tried to make the offensive linemen's job both easier and harder at the same time by introducing them to option blocking. Instead of squaring off as they had in the past with the opposite man and locking horns like two giant dinosaurs, the option blocker was expected to contact his opponent to determine the thrust of the opponent's drive and assist him in that direction; in other words, "take him in the direction he wants to go." Well, the back, reading the block of his offensive linemen, had that split-second choice to make his decision of which way to go, or, to run for daylight.

Lombardi's favorite play was the power sweep. Guards were assigned to pull and the running backs were expected to cut back, just as they had for Jock Sutherland's Pittsburgh teams against Fordham during Lombardi's playing days. Lombardi elaborated:

Every team eventually arrives at a lead play. It becomes the team's bread-and-butter play, the top-priority play. It is the play the team knows it must make go, and the one the opponents know they must stop. My number one play has been the power sweep. And there is nothing spectacular about it, it's just a yard gainer. But on that sideline, when the sweep starts to develop, you can hear those linebackers and defensive backs yelling, "Sweep! Sweep!" and almost see their eyes pop as those guards turn up field after them.

The ball carrier on the power sweep right is usually the halfback, and I've been fortunate to coach a couple of great all-around backs who made the sweep their personal play, Paul Hornung and Frank Gifford. Though neither had that blinding speed, they were both were quick, intelligent runners who could control their running so that they used their blockers and got every possible yard out of each play.

Though Lombardi's nucleus was stronger than he at first suspected, his talent still was too thin to win. Before the 1959 season, Lombardi made shrewd trades and free-agent pickups that gave the Packers instant respectability. Most of his trades not only paid quick dividends, but he also did not have to part with his most valuable players or draft choices. He traded linebacker Marv Matuzak to the Colts for left guard Fred (Fuzzy) Thurston, who had been with three teams but became a Packers fixture. "I was such a lost sheep, I thought for sure the Rams would get me next," Thurston cracked.

Safety Willie Wood, a star at Southern California, was not drafted because he was considered too small to play in the NFL. He had to write Lombardi to even get a tryout. Wood's five-foot-ten, 185-pound frame did not prevent him from making forty-eight interceptions, playing on all five of Lombardi's championship teams, and making the Hall of Fame. That move was just one of several that improved Lombardi's defense.

From the Browns, he acquired defensive end Bill Quinlan and halfback Lew Carpenter for end Billy Howton, a popular but declining

Packer star. He acquired defensive tackle Henry Jordan from the Browns for a fourth-round draft pick in 1960 and veteran star safety Emlen Tunnell from the Giants for cash. Quinlan, Jordan, and Wood all would start for Lombardi's first NFL championship team in 1961.

Lombardi's lack of front office experience obviously proved no hindrance for him, and the franchise's corporation, formerly a source of dysfunction, became a benefit. All profits were required to be plowed back into the corporation, and as the Packers started winning, profits were plentiful. Lombardi would have all the cash he needed to sign the best talent available. In 1959, he traded a future third-round pick to the Chicago Cardinals for quarterback Lamar McHan. "We've got a hell of a problem," he told Bengtson after studying film of the returning Packer quarterbacks. "We've got to find somebody who can move this club."

Lombardi, it turned out, was not always adept at spotting hidden gems. Starr, a future Hall of Fame quarterback, was sitting right under his nose. A seventeenth-round draft choice out of Alabama in 1956, Starr started in 1957 and threw three touchdown passes and twelve interceptions while splitting time with Babe Parilli in 1958. When Bengtson was asked to evaluate Starr, he told Lombardi, "He's adequate as a backup man, but other than that, I can't say too much for him. I certainly can't see him as a quarterback on a championship team."

Lombardi agreed and said, "I'll give him a fair look. But he's no Bobby Layne, no Dutch Van Brocklin."

Those two quarterbacks were fiery leaders, and Starr outwardly was not. Lombardi questioned whether Starr was "just a little too polite and maybe just a little too self-effacing" to be his quarterback. Little did he realize that Starr's temperament would prove the perfect complement to Lombardi's as they teamed up for one of the greatest rides in NFL history.

Starr first met Lombardi at a minicamp for quarterbacks in June 1959. Starr recalled,

I was very impressed from the first sessions he held with some of the offensive players. You had to know things were going to change because the leadership was so evident and that's what we were lacking. He was very tough but compared to my father, he was piece a cake. My dad was a tough master sergeant. It was marvelous working with him.

Yet Starr would not win over Lombardi for another season. In a defining moment of their relationship, Starr confronted his coach in his office after Lombardi chewed him out for an interception during practice. Starr recalled:

> The ball was tipped, it was not a clean interception. I told him not to chew me out in front of the team if he wants me to earn their respect. If he does it in the office, I can take the chewing, if I have it coming. But if later he sees he made an error and he apologizes in his office, he should apologize out there as well. He never, ever chewed me out in front of the team again.

McHan won the starting job in the Packers' last exhibition game of 1959. Lombardi did not consider him head and shoulders above Starr but suggested the team might benefit from a fresh face. "We need somebody different for the fans and opposition," Lombardi said upon naming McHan to start against the Chicago Bears in the opening game. Lombardi was a stickler for winning preseason games and as with most coaches taking over a loser, used them initially to foster a winning atmosphere. Though the Packers finished 4–2 in exhibitions, Lombardi confided to friends that he hoped his team could win that many games in the regular season.

The Packers' offense began the season sluggishly, getting no points out of three good first-half scoring opportunities against the Bears. But thanks to an inspired performance by their rebuilt defense, the Packers trailed just 6–0 midway through the fourth quarter. Second-year fullback Jim Taylor scored on a five-yard run, and the Packers led 7–6. A sixty-one-yard punt by McGee backed up the Bears at the two-yard line. Hanner tackled quarterback Ed Brown in the end zone for a safety, and the Lombardi era was off and winning. The sellout crowd of 32,150 excitedly counted down the final seconds, and the Packers carried Lombardi off the field. "We're on our way now!" he yelled in the joyful dressing room.

In one season, Lombardi obliterated the bad memories of eleven lost years. The Packers improved to 3–0 by beating the Detroit Lions 28-10 and the San Francisco 49ers 21–20. Sellout crowds in Green Bay cheered both wins. If this instant success seemed too good to be true, it was. The Packers were walloped 45–6 by the Los Angeles Rams at Milwaukee, the first of five straight losses. Four starters were knocked out of the lineup, including Taylor, who suffered severe burns while helping his wife put out a grease fire.

The Packers were outscored 131–47 during the first four losses. McHan was injured in a 20–3 loss to the New York Giants, and his replacement, Joe Francis, played poorly. McHan had to leave the next game, too, which resulted in a 28–17 loss to the Bears. Starr started the next week against the Baltimore Colts and played well enough in a 28–24 loss to keep the job when McHan was healthy again. "You are going to be our quarterback from here on out," Lombardi told Starr.

The Packers did not lose again in 1959. They defeated the Washington Redskins 21–0 at home to end their skid and then beat the Lions 24–17 in the traditional Thanksgiving game at Detroit. They beat the Rams in Los Angeles, 38–20, a fifty-seven-point swing from the loss that started their tailspin. They finished with a 36–14 road win over the San Francisco 49ers in which Starr had his finest performance yet. The Packers, 7–5, came home with their first winning record since 1947. Packer fans were delirious, and about 3,000 people met the team plane when it returned from Detroit on Thanksgiving. About 7,500 met the plane upon its return from San Francisco.

The Associated Press overwhelmingly voted Lombardi NFL Coach of the Year. He easily outpolled the Colts' Weeb Ewbank and the

Giants' Howell, who were preparing to meet in the NFL championship game for the second consecutive year. "I was hoping to win five games—tops," Lombardi said at a news conference announcing his award. "Seven was a surprise. Determination made the difference. I know it sounds corny, but that's the way it was."

Lombardi's success, however, left him in a quandary. Mara wanted him to return to the Giants and replace Howell, who said he was ready to retire. Mara reminded Olejniczak that he had agreed to let Lombardi out of his contract if Mara came calling. The Packers had a different recollection of their conversation and insisted they were not obliged to release Lombardi. They allowed him to negotiate with Mara, though, and Lombardi decided to stay in Green Bay while leaving the door open if Howell retired after the 1960 season. Lombardi received a $10,000 bonus for staying and used it to buy a mink coat for Marie. Allie Sherman replaced Howell in 1961.

The 1959 season laid the foundation for the Packer dynasty. Eight players with Lombardi that season were still in the starting lineup when his era ended with a 33–14 Super Bowl victory over the Oakland Raiders in January 1968. The Packers outgrew Lambeau Field's capacity, and it was expanded three times during the Lombardi years and again in 1970. A $295 million renovation started in 2001 increased the stadium to its current capacity of 72,928 seats.

The Lombardi legacy is never far from the hearts and minds of the Packers and their universal following. Even as the Packers in 1996 moved toward their first Super Bowl championship in twenty-nine years, some players wondered if the old coach and his players would have considered them worthy to carry the torch. "What people don't understand outside Green Bay," defensive end Sean Jones said, "is that we have to exorcise those ghosts: Willie Wood, Willie Davis, Bart Starr, Ray Nitschke. I think Ray Nitschke thinks we stink."

Lombardi, too, had a torch to carry. When he led the Packers to the inaugural Super Bowl against the Kansas City Chiefs in January 1967, he bore the added burden of upholding the NFL's honor. A loss to the

American Football League champions would disgrace not only Green Bay but the entire NFL, which considered the new league as inferior. And to think that when Lombardi left the Giants' sideline for the last time in 1958, the AFL was not even a gleam in Lamar Hunt's eye.

3

Lamar's League

It was in Lamar Hunt's heart, soul, and upbringing to believe that professional football could make its mark in Dallas. From early childhood, it seemed, he walked on a path that would lead him to form the American Football League. Put together in 1959, it remains the only success story among all the upstarts that have tried to take on the National Football League.

Hunt at first vacillated whether to pursue a professional baseball team or a professional football team for his hometown, Dallas. When he joined some fifty million Americans watching the Baltimore Colts defeat the New York Giants on December 28, 1958, his mind was made up. "My interest emotionally was always more in football," Hunt told Michael MacCambridge in *America's Game*. "But clearly, the '58 Colts-Giants game, sort of in my mind, made me say, 'Well, that's it. This sport really has everything. And it televises well.' And who knew what that meant?"

That observation steered Hunt toward the NFL, which turned him away and unwittingly steered him to a new league. Establishing a second league seemed a reasonable proposition, except that nobody had pulled that off in forty years. College football provided a near-bottomless pool of professional-caliber players and coaches. No football league has failed because it ran out of players. Thanks to the NFL's reluctance to expand, untapped football markets were plentiful in 1959. Cities enjoying a postwar boom wanted sports teams to show off their civic pride and prosperity. A professional franchise, in more ways than one, could put a city in the big leagues.

Some of the most promising pro football markets had been part of the All-America Football Conference (AAFC). Formed in 1946, it fought the good fight against the NFL, yet folded after four seasons. The new league competed directly with the NFL in New York, Chicago, and Los Angeles. It filled open markets in Baltimore, Buffalo, Cleveland, Miami, and San Francisco. But in the end, the new league had more foresight than money. When it failed after the 1949 season, the NFL absorbed three of its franchises. The most notable of these was the Cleveland Browns, which went on to become NFL champions in 1950. Had all the AAFC owners had deep enough pockets to hold on a few more years, the league might well have gotten over the hump. As the Browns showed, a new league did not have to settle for second-class talent. And when the AFL got organized, a decade after the AAFC's demise, television's role as a new league's lifesaver was becoming more promising.

Hunt, the son of billionaire Dallas oilman H. L. Hunt, had little interest in devoting his life to the oil business. Instead, he was drawn to sports promotion, an outgrowth of his fascination with competition. As a youngster, he created all sorts of diversions and kept meticulous records. This pastime earned him the nickname "Games," which he actually deserved for the rest of his life. Hunt would invent games to break the tedium of family car trips and vacations at the beach, which the rest of his family enjoyed far more than he. "When we got to the beach, we'd have the 'family Olympics,'" Hunt's widow, Norma, recalled. "He'd organize and create games—putting contests, shooting baskets ... especially for the youngest children. Everybody competed. My parents competed. He'd have this huge raft of people he'd have to keep the stats on. We'd compete every day. That made him happy."

Football, however, was the game that made Hunt happiest. "When he was just a child, his family took him to the first Cotton Bowl," said Norma Hunt, referring to the 1938 game, when Lamar was five years old.

> He had about a sixty-year string of going to Cotton Bowl games. So he was seeing major college football at the highest level from the earliest years of his life. He sat on the bench at SMU and saw some very good teams with big crowds. Everything about Lamar's experience with football in Dallas told him the city could support a pro football team.

Texas was famous for the passion of its high school and college football fans when Hunt formed the AFL. So he was naturally drawn to oilman K. S. (Bud) Adams, whom Hunt recruited to place a team in Houston and start a rivalry with Hunt's team in Dallas. Yet the NFL in early 1959 had no interest in either city or in any other available market. The established league had fluctuated between ten and thirteen teams since 1933, and it wanted no part of Dallas. The NFL placed the Texans there in 1952, only to see them finish 1–11, go broke, and dump the franchise back on the league. Hunt was not willing to let that failure stand for his hometown's pro football potential, however, and would, of course, name his team "the Texans."

Norma Hunt said,

> Rejection by the NFL? They simply told the wrong guy they weren't going to give him a franchise. One thing that is totally underplayed is Lamar's competitiveness. He was one of the most competitive people I've ever known. He had that kind, low-key, unassuming, humble nature. But he really had a core of steel. He wanted to win. He knew there were cities and potential owners who should have pro football teams. If you told him that isn't going to happen, that wasn't logical to him. Other cities and their fans deserved to have teams.

Hunt was only twenty-six years old when he decided to form the AFL. With a slim build and horn-rim glasses, he seemed an unlikely revolutionary. He could be difficult to read and easy to underestimate. Hunt was so unpretentious that he kept his home phone number listed in the Dallas directory until he died on December 13, 2006, at age seventy-four. He started out in the family business, the Hunt Oil Company, after graduating from Southern Methodist University in 1955 with a degree in geology.

Although he played college football, Hunt did not earn a varsity football letter at SMU, mainly because he sat behind three receivers who went on to the NFL. They included Raymond Berry, who became a Hall of Fame receiver with the Baltimore Colts. Berry recalled,

> We were classmates and teammates and played the same position. He was a heck of an athlete. But getting on the field at SMU was tough because there were too many great athletes. Lamar was a real great guy to be around. He was very likable—none of us really knew about his wealth. He was really like everybody else. He had always shown a lot of smarts. I wouldn't be surprised by anything Lamar had done. He was always a low-profile, under-the-radar-type person. But he always knew what he was doing. I guess he did, didn't he?

Hunt first considered investing in baseball when former MLB executive Branch Rickey began recruiting franchises for the Continental League in 1958. Hunt joined a group of Dallas–Fort Worth investors who listened to a Rickey sales pitch in New York. The Continental League was formally announced July 27, 1959, and though it never materialized, Rickey's impact on Hunt was profound. Hunt caught expansion fever and absorbed Rickey's plan to share the wealth. Rickey proposed that owners in his league would equally split two-thirds of their television revenues.

Hunt was keeping his sports options open and earlier that year had asked NFL commissioner Bert Bell if he might acquire a franchise for Dallas. Bell replied that the league had no plans to expand. He suggested that Hunt contact Walter and Violet Wolfner, who owned the Chicago Cardinals and had been fielding offers. The Cardinals, willed to Violet Wolfner by her late husband, Charles Bidwill, were a poor relation to the Bears. They habitually lost money and had just one winning season since 1949.

Several NFL owners wanted the Cardinals to move, especially the Bears' coach and owner, George Halas. According to league policy, telecasts of NFL home games were blacked out, and because the Bears and Cardinals alternated home dates, their away games could not be shown in Chicago. Halas had the far more marketable team, and this arrangement cost him money and exposure. Bell was holding back on expansion until the league's perennial losers became more competitive. The outlook for a Cardinals' turnaround would improve if they found a new owner or city, but the Wolfners wanted to keep their options open. As long as the NFL stayed with twelve teams, the Cardinals' value would be inflated. But since they also pondered a move, the Wolfners did not want an expansion team moving into a market they might want. As one suitor after another came to realize, the Wolfners wanted a partner who would pump cash into their team while they remained majority owners. Hunt was the last in a parade of rejected suitors.

Hunt met with the Wolfners for the last time at their winter home in Miami early in 1959. Though the deal fell through, his time had been well spent. The Wolfners told him about others with whom they had negotiated, notably Adams in Houston and a group in Minneapolis. It dawned on Hunt that he had been talking to the wrong people. As Hunt recalled in Jeff Miller's *Going Long,*

> The thought just occurred to me. I've heard about all of these
> people that want to buy the Cardinals and move them. Why
> wouldn't it be possible to form a second league? Later, I

kiddingly said it was like the light bulb coming on over your head. I can remember sitting in that airplane when it dawned on me that that was maybe a better alternative.

When he boarded an American Airlines flight from Miami to Dallas, Hunt's bulb became brighter. He asked a flight attendant for stationery and on three sheets wrote in small, meticulous letters a business plan for a new league. Most of what he learned about professional sports during the previous year was condensed into that plan. From Rickey, he learned sound principles for starting a league. The Wolfners opened their books to him, allowing him to grasp what it would take for a pro football franchise to break even. Using the National Hockey League as a model, he planned for six teams. His cities were hypothetical, and after a four-hour flight, Hunt's proposal for a league looked like this:

Original Six—First Year's Operation

1) 15-game schedule (three have eight at home, three have only seven)—play each team three times with clubs splitting net gate after visitors are paid for travel expenses
2) Three exhibition games
3) Split net gate 60% to home—40% to visitor with visitors having a choice of 40% or $35,000, whichever is greater
4) Draft

    (A)Territorial Rights—each club shall have the right to two territorial choices before draft starts. Territory shall comprise the state in which the club is located. If there are two clubs in a state, closest by mileage to college where player performed shall have rights. After making a territorial choice, or choices, club shall lose its position in first or second rounds of draft depending on whether two choices are made.

    (B) There shall be 30 rounds of the draft

(C) Clubs shall draw for positions of draft and first 10 rounds should be thus, i.e., (1) Los Angeles, (2) Denver, (3) Dallas, (4) Houston, (5) Buffalo, (6) New York, (7) New York, (8) Buffalo, (9) Houston, (10) Dallas, (11) Denver, (12) Los Angeles—each club getting two players. At the end of the 10th and 20th rounds, a fresh draw will re-determine the order of draw. At end of draft, each club will have drafted 60 players.

5) League will get 3% of net gate (after stadium)

6) League Dues—$1,000

7) League will make all stadium contracts rather than individual clubs

8) All TV and radio must be league approved

9) TV money will go 1/3rd to individual clubs and 2/3rd to league

10) League will have offices in New York

11) League will have commissioner and FBI assistant [a former agent to oversee league security] and publicity man

12) Each owner will loan the league $200,000 for five years, interest free, at the end of which time the money will be returned to owners if they feel it is advisable. If any owner returns his franchise before five years, he shall forfeit his earnest money.

13) During the first year of operation, each owner shall maintain a working account of $200,000 (this shall begin with first exhibition game and end January 31). League shall be notified by bank for failure to comply with this.

14) 27 or 28 player limit with a payroll limit of $252,000 for regular season games

15) No requirement as to net worth of owners but merely to their ability to stand tax loss of $200,000/year for five years (must have gross income of $300,000 with prospect that it will continue).

16) Pension plan to follow NFL

17) All-Star Game in either Dallas or Houston one or two weeks after championship game

18) Championship game between division leaders in city deemed best from stadium and climate factors

19) No players shall play in this league who have contractual obligations in either Canada or U.S.

20) No club should have more than three stockholders with at least one required to own 50%

21) At league meetings only one representative will be allowed for each club, i.e., one stockholder plus general manager, if desired

22) League will operate under framework of NFL in all cases not excepted here

23) Commissioner—five-year contract at same (salary) as NFL with same powers

24) All clubs submit all financial reports to league with none to be publicly released

First Season

Income:

6 home games, 25,000 average attendance	=$150,000
	x $4
	$600,000
Rental	-90,000
League	-10,200
	499,800
4 exhibition games, 10,000 average attendance	= 40,000
	x $3.50
	$140,000
To promoters	47,000
	= 93,000
½	46,500

Assumed no TV   0

                                                          546,300

Expenses:

Payroll exhibitions only (40 players)	$8,000
Players Payroll (28 x $9,000)	252,000
Coaches (Limit)	40,000
Trainer	5,000
Business Manager	15,000
Publicity Man	7,500
2 secretaries	10,000
Training camp 50 Players x $10 x 50 days	
(counts exhibitions)	25,000
Equipment $500 x 50 Players	25,000
Travel: Assuming 10 trips Equal to Dallas–	
New York $150 x 33 x 10	=49,500
Hotels & Meals $12/Day x 2 Days x 10 Trips x 33	=7,920
Travel to and from camp for those cut $100 x 20	2,000
Balls 100 x $30	=3,000
Ticket Costs	5,000
Pictures (Game) $300 x 16	=4,800
Publicity	6,000
Office rent	5,000

                                                          470,720

Office supplies (stationery, stamps, etc.)   10,000
League dues   5,000

League income

$40,800 from league games

$5,000 dues + 2/3 of TV income of each club

"That, by today's standards, was not a very well-developed plan," said Norma Hunt. "But you could see the genius in it. Lamar loved numbers and you can see how many numbers were in it. He was a brilliant mathematician. He had a friend who taught math and he told me that Lamar's mathematical ability just blew him away."

The key to Hunt's audacious plan was his unflagging faith, not the numbers. "He was, literally, one of the most positive people who ever lived," Norma Hunt said. "He just believed. There was so little negativism in Lamar's thought process—ever. And he had absolutely a passion for the sport—beyond everything that maybe a lot of people could have ever imagined. He just believed it was the greatest game, and he couldn't see enough games."

Hunt was not yet ready to burn his bridges with the NFL, however, and again asked Bell about acquiring a Dallas franchise. Bell replied that the league would not expand until the Cardinals decided whether to move. Halas, who with Pittsburgh Steelers owner Art Rooney headed the NFL expansion committee, discouraged Hunt, too.

Adams, who had received a similar runaround from the NFL, was all ears when Hunt approached him about forming a new league. More boisterous and less ingratiating than Hunt was, Adams was a former University of Kansas football player, the son of Phillips Petroleum board chairman "Boots" Adams, and the founder of the ADA Oil Company. Adams's Houston Oilers would win the first two AFL championships. "He was one of the main reasons the AFL succeeded, particularly in trades, scouting players and signing [top] players," Hunt said. "He always did his best to boost our image. I can't say enough great things about him."

When the two first met, Adams, then thirty-six years old, mirrored Hunt in financial resources and football experience. Adams had attended Culver Military Academy, an Indiana prep school, with Lamar's brother Nelson Bunker Hunt, who later arranged a meeting with Adams and Lamar. They met at a Houston steakhouse Adams owned, and Adams quickly realized Hunt often did not come right to the point. Adams recalled,

Lamar was somewhat shy then. We talked about everything, but I couldn't figure out what he wanted. I drove him back to the airport, and we were about two blocks away when he said, "I know you tried to buy the Cardinals. I did, too. . . . Would you be interested in starting a new league up?" I said, "Yeah, I would."

Hunt next called Willard Rhodes in Seattle, who wanted a franchise, but the University of Washington would not let him use its Husky Stadium. The Minneapolis group that had negotiated with the Wolfners came on board, though. So did Bob Howsam, a minor-league baseball owner in Denver who, like Hunt, had been interested in the Continental League. Howsam said,

> He called me out of the clear blue and said he'd like to come to Denver and visit with me about sports. When he came up, he talked to me about the American Football League. Denver was a great sports city to begin with, plus the fact we had a new stadium and wanted to add some entertainment and keep it fully occupied.

Bob Howsam Jr. remembers his father's exploratory talks with Hunt.

> I remember vacating my bedroom, and it was kind of like "George Washington slept here." I heard the reputation about all this oil money, but he was such a regular guy. My mom cooked up a meal, and he was just so gracious and generous. I think he really appreciated my father lending his sports experience. He had this trench-like experience in sports and a sense of the big picture.

Hunt now had four owners but knew that any new league needed the major markets of New York and Los Angeles. He had a New York connection in Bill Shea, a lawyer who had teamed up with Rickey to promote the Continental League. When that league fell through, Shea helped New York acquire the Mets, a National League expansion team. Its permanent home, Shea Stadium, was named for him. Shea referred Hunt to Harry Wismer, a popular New York sportscaster and a minority owner in both the Washington Redskins and Detroit Lions. Wismer jumped on board. Hunt recruited hotel owner Barron Hilton to take the Los Angeles franchise, thanks to an introduction from Gene Mako, a well-known tennis pro and avid pro football fan who lived in Los Angeles.

Hunt's journey when forming the new league was filled with puzzling starts and stops. He flew to Philadelphia in early June to ask Bell one more time if the NFL might expand to Dallas. Hunt was rebuffed again, and in July, through an intermediary, he notified Bell that he planned to start a new league. Hunt asked Bell if he might serve as commissioner of both leagues, as did baseball commissioner Ford Frick for the American League and National League. It apparently did not dawn on Hunt that NFL owners most likely would have fired Bell before they would allow him to help launch a competing league.

It was Bell, oddly enough, who announced the new league's formation on July 28, 1959. Bell was trying to convince a Senate sub-committee that the NFL should have an antitrust exemption identical to that of Major League Baseball and felt he could use the declaration of a new league to his advantage. With Hunt in attendance, Bell tried to quell the government's concerns that the NFL sought to monopolize pro football, and he lauded the proposed AFL. "The more football there is and the more advertisement of pro football, the better off we are," Bell said. He claimed that NFL owners were "all for the new league and would help nurture it."

After the hearings, Hunt visited Bell on his farm near Atlantic City. No longer pestering him to expand, Hunt wanted reassurance that the NFL would not pursue that option. Bell told him the NFL would not expand until it improved its competitive balance from top to bottom, which probably would take several years. If his assertion was true, four of Hunt's six franchises would have the only game in town. Hunt was ready to move.

He and Adams met in Houston on August 3 to officially announce the AFL's formation, with Houston and Dallas as the founding franchises. The six owners met August 14 at the Chicago Hilton and agreed to name their venture the American Football League and to begin play in 1960. The owners met again in Dallas on August 22 and approved a rule book and articles of association. Each agreed to put up a $100,000 performance bond and contribute $25,000 earnest money.

NFL owners soon made it clear that when Bell welcomed the new league in Washington, he was not speaking for them. Before a Steelers-Bears exhibition game August 29 in Houston, Halas and Rooney held a press conference to announce NFL plans for expansion in 1961, most likely to Dallas and Houston. They also said the NFL was considering Boston, Buffalo, Denver, Miami, Minneapolis, Louisville, and New Orleans. That meant potential competition in every AFL city. Given the NFL's repeated opposition to expansion, this announcement came as a bombshell. Adding insult to injury, Adams had promoted the Steelers-Bears exhibition game.

Hunt said,

> Everybody has been knocking on their door for years and they've turned everybody down. It is obvious what they are trying to do, and it can get them in trouble. They're trying to knock out Dallas and Houston, but this doesn't change our plans at all and we're moving ahead. We'll be adding our seventh and eighth teams this fall.

Not all NFL owners welcomed the announcement in Houston. George Preston Marshall of the Redskins told the *New York Daily Mirror*: "The only reason I've heard from other owners is that we could destroy the new league. If that's the only reason, then we are guilty of monopolistic practices. No one can give me an intelligent reason for adding a couple more franchises."

But it was clear to most NFL owners that pro football was going to new markets with or without them. And Halas feared the AFL had a better chance to survive than the All-America Football Conference. "[Hunt] was a formidable rival," Halas wrote. "His oil money gave him a rare ability to absorb losses for a long time and to support other teams." Hunt cautioned fellow owners that they would have to withstand heavy initial losses. When H. L. Hunt was asked after the AFL's maiden season how long his son could keep losing $1 million a year, he replied that at that rate, Lamar would go broke in another 150 years. But contrary to Halas's claim, Hunt did not subsidize the entire league.

Lamar Hunt's wealth does not begin to explain why, of all the new pro football leagues, only his succeeded. The World Football League, United States Football League, and XFL all have failed since then. The USFL included some immensely wealthy owners, including Donald Trump, and the XFL had the NBC television network as its partner. Money alone did not get a league off the ground. With the AFL, Hunt also needed the resolve to undertake overwhelming work and travel and the courage and savvy to stand up to the NFL's old guard.

Norma Hunt, who married Lamar in 1964, said,

> He engaged in productive activity virtually all the time. To him, work, pleasure and play were all the same. He did not want down time. He did not feel stress like other people feel it. He was always calm in the interior of his being. He thought that no matter how bad the problem was, he could work hard enough to solve it.

Nobody tested Hunt in the football jungle more severely than Halas did. He constantly tried to seduce Hunt and Adams away from their partners by offering them the NFL franchises they had sought in the first place. During the summer of 1959, before Hunt and his partners fully committed to a new league, Halas invited Hunt and Adams to his sporting goods store in downtown Chicago. Howsam was asked to come along and listened as Halas offered Hunt an NFL team in Dallas and Adams one in Houston. That offer violated NFL bylaws, which required a vote by all owners to approve expansion.

"They were trying to break up the AFL," Adams said. "He thought if he could get two guys out of there, we couldn't start a new league. And he probably was right. Halas tried very hard to persuade us not to start this new league. He said it would be very costly and wouldn't be good for pro football."

Halas told Howsam the NFL had no interest in Denver, but Halas offered to help him buy a share of any NFL team. Howsam had built the Denver Bears into a thriving minor-league baseball franchise and was not interested in a franchise elsewhere. Halas's visitors told him they would consider his offer.

Howsam reflected,

> I'm not sure why, but Halas hated Denver. I guess he thought it would not do well. So we went back to the hotel and they said, "Well, what do you think?" I said, "I'd like to have Denver. It's my home. I understand you two can have franchises, so I'll accept whatever you decide." After quite a bit of discussion, they said, "We're sticking with you." They rejected Halas's offer. I've always had such great respect for Lamar and Bud for doing that.

Halas's pessimism about Denver seemed justified. Neither Denver daily newspaper sent a reporter to the AFL's organizational meeting in mid-August to cover the city's admission. The *Rocky Mountain News* covered the event with only a six-paragraph wire service story, which was headlined: "It's Official! Denver in New Grid Pro Loop." The newspapers' snubs frustrated Howsam. He recalled,

It was tough in those days to get any coverage. The two papers wouldn't give us great support. I served on committees with their editors and publishers quite a lot and they told me, "Bob, we're not going to support you or send anybody with the ball club until you prove you can get the job done." Of course, if you got the NFL, they would have supported you immediately. When you're trying to get it started, that's when you need the support.

The AFL added a Buffalo franchise, owned by Ralph Wilson, on October 28, 1959. A part-owner of the Detroit Lions, Wilson originally wanted an AFL franchise in Miami, but the University of Miami would not share the use of the Orange Bowl. A Boston group, led by Billy Sullivan, became the AFL's eighth franchise on November 16.

The AFL held its first draft November 22, 1959, in Minneapolis and featured territorial picks to allow franchises to pick college stars with regional appeal. Hunt took Southern Methodist University (SMU) quarterback Don Meredith. Houston took Louisiana State University (LSU) running back Billy Cannon, who would win the Heisman Trophy. The NFL's Los Angeles Rams also drafted Cannon first overall, and the competition to sign him kicked off a war between the leagues.

The AFL draft was highly unorthodox. As Hunt described it,

We had a committee of knowledgeable football people, and there were only two or three associated with the league. But they ranked the eight best quarterbacks in the draft, and those eight were picked out of a hat. We ranked the eight best centers, and those were picked out of a hat, one to a team. So literally, our choices were pulled out of the hat. Meredith also was one of the eight best quarterbacks, so we did not get another quarterback in that portion of the draft.

Little did Hunt realize that trouble was afoot. When Hunt and Adams turned down Halas, NFL emissaries continued wooing other

AFL owners throughout the late summer and fall. The Rams' Ed Pauley told Hilton he could buy into that franchise. Halas was persistent in his entreaties to Hunt and Adams, and Hunt finally replied that he would drop the AFL only if the NFL accepted all its franchises. Halas refused. He still did not want Denver or competition for NFL teams in New York and Los Angeles.

Once Hunt was committed to forging ahead, he threw a jab at Halas and his partners. "Unless the NFL folds," he said, "there will be two professional football leagues next year."

Halas had yet another trick up his sleeve, however. And this one worked. He offered an NFL franchise to the AFL's Minneapolis group of H. P. Skoglund, William Boyer, Max Winter, and Ole Haugsrud. Minneapolis became an NFL expansion target when a suitable home stadium could not be found for an NFL franchise in Houston. Before the AFL draft, the Minneapolis group accepted Halas's deal.

"Of course, he was used to getting his way," Howsam said. "He was trying to destroy the AFL. You never feel good about something like that. They did leave and we went about making our league as successful as we could."

While AFL owners sat down in Minneapolis, news of the local group's defection broke in the *Minneapolis Star Tribune*. This timing was exquisite for Halas because college players about to be drafted might be convinced that the new league was collapsing. Wismer was the first AFL owner to see the story about the pullout and angrily entered a dinner reception for the owners. Wismer said this event was the "last supper" and called Winter a "Judas." Skoglund denied the report, though it was confirmed when he and his partners asked the AFL to return their $25,000 earnest money.

This defector, ironically, had recently recruited the AFL's first commissioner. Skoglund was the major investor in Raven Industries, a South Dakota company that manufactured high-altitude research balloons, and had invited company vice president Joe Foss to join him on the company plane to Los Angeles. Both checked into the Beverly

Hilton, where Foss was staying on Raven business and Skoglund was attending an AFL meeting. Before Foss went to his room, Skoglund invited him to a cocktail party with the new league's owners. Foss had been a reserve lineman at the University of South Dakota, but he was best known for serving two terms as South Dakota's governor and for receiving the Congressional Medal of Honor for his legendary record as a World War II fighter pilot.

Foss dropped by the party and learned the AFL needed a commissioner, preferably one with a high profile and a knack for promotion. Foss was asked if he would be interested in the job and agreed to be interviewed. "I loved football, both playing and watching it," he wrote, "so the thought of being a commissioner of one of my favorite sports certainly had its appeal." When Foss was interviewed the next evening, some owners belittled his thin football résumé. He countered:

> Seems to me what you need is somebody who has the ability to open doors and pump life into a dead horse. From what I've heard, the National Football League has a forty-year head start and right now you're being confused with the new Continental baseball league that's trying to get started. If you're going to be successful, you've got to have somebody who's willing to travel the length and breadth of this land and talk to people in person and get attention for the league.

Foss doubted he would be asked back for a follow-up session. The next day's *Los Angeles Times* quoted Thomas Eddy, Hilton's aide with the Chargers, as saying the AFL is "certain of one thing and that is that Joe Foss will not be commissioner." Foss told Skoglund he no longer wanted the job. A few weeks later, however, Hunt asked Foss to reconsider and to join a conference call with Hunt, Adams, and Howsam. They offered Foss a three-year contract at $30,000 a year, and he officially was hired November 30. The AFL now had a commissioner who was always willing to talk up the new league and loved a good fight.

Almost lost amid the November turmoil was the most important decision in the history of the AFL and, arguably, of pro football. During their intrigue-filled weekend, the AFL owners agreed they would equally share television revenues. This pronouncement was not then considered a big deal—it was anybody's guess if the new league's TV rights fees would amount to a hill of beans—but that agreement would assure the AFL's survival and turn pro football into America's most popular and profitable sport.

In that decision, AFL owners were remarkable for their consensus and vision. Many sports executives, particularly those in Major League Baseball, considered revenue sharing radical and even "socialist." Hunt received a primer in revenue sharing of broadcast revenues during his flirtation with the Continental League and initially wanted to borrow Rickey's formula in which each team would keep one-third of its television money and equally share the rest. He and his partners eventually decided it would be simpler just to equally split all the television money.

Hunt seemed an unlikely champion of revenue sharing. He was, after all, supposed to be a Texas oil baron who conducted business on the premise that only the strongest survive. He had the foresight, however, to realize cutthroat competition with his partners was not the right approach for starting a new league. Norma Hunt said,

> Lamar often said to me, "Any league is only as strong as its weakest link." You need everybody to succeed. Everybody can't be New York. Therefore, you've got to address that in very positive ways. Revenue sharing obviously was the way to do it. It's one of the most important decisions ever. It's still the key to the success of the NFL fifty years later.

Despite the terrific ratings for the telecast of the 1958 NFL championship game, television production of sports was still in the leather-helmet era. The AFL was quick to embrace changes in broadcasting and exposed the NFL as complacent. The AFL would make the game easier to watch by sewing the players' last names on the backs of their jerseys, a recent innovation of Chicago White Sox owner Bill Veeck. AFL teams would have the option of kicking an extra point or running or passing for two points after a touchdown. The scoreboard would also serve as the official game clock and avoid the confusion of the NFL, where the official time was kept on the field but not synchronized with the scoreboard. The AFL also would let the network cameras show fights and arguments, which were off limits in the NFL.

Foss spoke forcefully for the AFL's innovations, and his war record gave him instant credibility. Reporters liked to compare his missions as a fighter pilot to his fight against the NFL. One even asked Foss what he would do if he spotted Halas flying a Japanese Zero fighter plane. Foss was only too happy to play along. Asked at his first news conference if the AFL would allow cameras to show fights on the field, he replied, "I really haven't thought about it, but you never get anywhere backing away from a fight. It's all right with me."

Foss and the NFL continually traded jabs. He said,

> During my first month as skipper of the new league, the press relished a series of subtly hostile exchanges with George Halas, the NFL's leading critic of the AFL. But even that kept us in the public eye, and we needed public interest in the league. I had something going every day for the sportswriters to jangle about, and I loved every minute of it.

With the loss of Minneapolis, the league had seven teams, lists of drafted players to sign, and a commissioner. Finding coaches was the next order of business. Hunt wanted to hire a coach who would turn heads in Dallas. He started at the top of the pile, approaching legendary University of Oklahoma coach Bud Wilkinson. Hunt also approached Tom Landry, a former star at the University of Texas. Landry's success coaching the New York Giants' defense had made him pro football's hottest coaching prospect, and Tex Schramm, president of the proposed

NFL franchise in Dallas, was already courting him. Both Landry and Wilkinson turned down Hunt.

He next approached Hank Stram, the University of Miami's offensive backfield coach, who had served on the SMU staff soon after Hunt's playing days. Hunt had visited Stram in the spring of 1959, though he seemed a long shot as a pro coaching candidate. On the one hand, Stram wasn't even considered a hot prospect for a head coaching job in college football. On the other hand, any coach going to the new league might be committing career suicide. Stram was willing to take that risk.

"It turned out to be a very lucky selection on my part," Hunt said. "It was his personality and the fact he wanted the job. It was very apparent he wanted to be a head coach. He had a very good reputation as far as offensive football. He was a good teacher. He knew how to describe things and articulate what he wanted."

Stram wanted the job badly enough to overlook Hunt's quirks, including his exasperating habit of beating around the bush. Stram recalled in his autobiography that he was at a football banquet in his hometown of Gary, Indiana, after the 1959 season when Hunt phoned and asked him to fly to Dallas the next morning. Stram rushed to Dallas, but Hunt only seemed interested in reminiscing about the Mustangs' glory days. Stram was getting edgy and reminded Hunt that he had to catch a plane to Chicago for another banquet. He finally asked Hunt if he'd called to discuss a coaching job. "Ah, I . . . we'd like you to be the head football coach," Hunt replied.

Hunt offered to drive his new coach to the airport but asked Stram if he would walk six blocks to get Hunt's car while he made a few more phone calls. When Stram reached the lot, he looked for a luxury car befitting a wealthy Texan, but an attendant pointed him to a battered Oldsmobile. When Stram double-checked whether it actually was Hunt's car, the attendant said he was positive because he'd been trying to buy it from Hunt for $600. "He wants eight [hundred] and won't take less," the attendant said. "We've been haggling for weeks."

During their first interview in Miami, Hunt invited Stram to dinner. But when the check arrived, Hunt had no money, and Stram had to pay. This incident was just one of countless stories about Hunt lacking the cash to pay for a meal, cab fare, or even a highway toll. When he visited the Stram home after dinner and propped up his feet, the coach and his wife, Phyllis, were amused to see holes in Hunt's soles.

"I did need to keep a very close eye on Lamar's wardrobe," Norma Hunt said, laughing.

> He would not spend two minutes buying clothes. He hated it. He was way too busy for that. He wanted comfortable shoes but it's hard to get them for somebody if they don't try them on. Finally, I said, "I'll just buy everything else and if you just go to buy shoes, I'll go with you." Early in our marriage, we got to New York City and Lamar didn't have close to what we needed to pay the cab driver. Fortunately, I had enough to squeak by with the little he had. From then on, it was, "Go to the bank and get a whole lot of money," if you were going somewhere with Lamar. He had much better things to do with his money, like founding leagues, which cost a fortune. But the smaller amounts he just didn't have.

As 1959 came to a close, Hunt and his partners had not replaced the Minneapolis franchise and needed an eighth team for a balanced schedule. Atlanta and Oakland emerged as top candidates with Miami and St. Louis—about to become the Cardinals' new home—also under consideration. The AFL chose the Oakland group led by local business-man Chet Soda. His team could provide a Los Angeles–Oakland rivalry, similar to the one Hunt and Adams were forging in Texas. Oakland was given the Minneapolis draft picks and allowed to pick five unprotected players from each AFL team.

The Oakland group's eight investors included Wayne Valley, whose legacy would include coining the nickname for the AFL owners who started play in 1960. He joked that the eight partners should be known as the "Foolish Club." Hunt appropriated that nickname and made it famous. "I was an amateur photographer and had taken some color pictures of the sixty-four season," he recalled. "I sent out a montage as Christmas gifts one year. At the top was the hand-lettered phrase, 'The Foolish Club.'"

The members did not always get along. Wismer, a heavy drinker given to erratic behavior, fought with Foss from the start. Though the decision to hire Foss was announced as unanimous, Wismer opposed him. He questioned Foss's football background and called him a "hick." Foss upset the other AFL owners, too, when he agreed to return the $25,000 earnest money to the Minneapolis group. Most owners agreed that should have been forfeited.

The Minneapolis defection would cause bad blood between the leagues for at least a decade. Hunt was not one to hold a grudge, yet he gained a huge measure of satisfaction when his Kansas City Chiefs defeated the Minnesota Vikings 23–7 in the January 1970 Super Bowl. The victory held extra meaning for Hunt because though the leagues had merged in 1966, it was the last season in which the AFL played as a separate entity.

As Norma Hunt recalled,

> Max Winter was bought off and that was very devastating to the remaining guys. It made the Super Bowl even much sweeter and one of the strangest things happened. We were staying in the same hotel in New Orleans [as the Winters] and didn't know they were there. The day of the game, we were leaving and the Winters and Hunts were the only ones on the elevator—that wouldn't happen again in a million years.

Norma Hunt recalled the Winters seemed ill at ease. Perhaps they still felt awkward about bolting the AFL. Or perhaps they were just uptight about the big game, though the Vikings were heavy favorites.

The couples made small talk, but the Hunts became energized by their rivals' apprehension.

"We came off the elevator feeling they were extremely nervous," Norma Hunt said. "We looked at each other and said, 'We're going to win. If they're frightened, we're in good shape.' We can't say enough about the other guys. It wasn't just Lamar who hung tough. They all hung. And it was tough."

4

Showdown in Dallas

Lamar Hunt started the American Football League with the assumption that he would have Dallas all to himself. For National Football League rivals hoping to kill the new league in the cradle, though, the Texans were their inevitable target. From the start, consequently, Hunt faced a formidable adversary in his own backyard.

Even before they officially had a franchise, the Dallas Cowboys boasted wealthy owners, an experienced general manager, and pro football's hottest young coach, Tom Landry. He spent his last game as a New York Giants assistant coach when they faced the Colts in Baltimore for the NFL championship on December 27, 1959. An eagerly anticipated rematch of "The Greatest Game Ever Played," it proved a weak sequel.

The Giants led 9–7 into the fourth quarter, thanks to Pat Summerall's three field goals. Landry's defense was burned early by a fifty-nine-yard bomb from John Unitas to halfback Lenny Moore, but otherwise it held the Colts' explosive offense in check. The Giants seemed primed to take charge when they sat inches away from a first down at the Baltimore Colts' twenty-eight-yard line, but halfback Alex Webster was stopped short on fourth down by defensive end Gino Marchetti, who had also made a pivotal fourth-down tackle of Frank Gifford the year before.

The Colts made short work of Landry's farewell to New York. They ran off twenty-four straight points for a 31–16 victory. Unitas scored on a four-yard run to give the Colts a 14–9 lead. Giants quarterback Charlie Conerly threw three interceptions, including one returned forty-two yards for a touchdown by cornerback Johnny Sample. Weeb Ewbank's Colts were on top of the NFL again. Landry soon would be at the bottom. That same day, he officially accepted Tex Schramm's offer to become head coach in waiting of the NFL expansion team in Dallas. Schramm was still a CBS assistant director of sports in New York while serving as president and general manager of the Dallas team. Both he and Landry would leave New York for Dallas and change NFL history.

Commanding the sideline with a snap-brim hat, a suit, and stone-faced expression, Landry became the signature figure for one of the most storied teams ever. The Cowboys, with five Super Bowl appearances, a bevy of star players, sexy cheerleaders, and a worldwide following, helped boost pro football's glamour and television ratings to unprecedented levels. NFL Films gave the title *America's Team* to his Cowboys' 1978 highlights film, and the nickname still sticks.

Landry joined the Giants in 1950 as a cornerback and punter and added assistant coach duties in 1954. When he retired as a player, Coach Jim Lee Howell asked Landry to take over the defense in 1956. The Giants climaxed that season with a 47–7 victory over the Chicago Bears in the NFL championship game. Landry's defense helped the Giants reach three title games in four years, and Howell called him "the greatest football coach in the game today."

Schramm was general manager of the Los Angeles Rams before moving to CBS, and he had been on the lookout for the right opportunity to get back in the NFL. Clint Murchison Jr. and Bedford Wynne, co-owners of a team expecting admission to the NFL, presented one in October 1959. While living in New York, Schramm could not help but appreciate Landry's achievements. "People were calling him a young genius for what he'd done with the Giants' defense," Schramm said in his biography. "For the first time anybody could remember, the crowd was giving the defense a standing ovation, instead of the offense." When Giants co-owner Wellington Mara realized he could not keep Landry in New York, he encouraged Schramm to hire him. Landry agreed to a personal services contract to coach the Dallas team as soon as it joined the NFL.

"I wasn't surprised," said Landry, who, at thirty-five years old, became the NFL's youngest head coach.

> Our defense at New York had been very successful, and Vince Lombardi had recently gone from our staff to the head job at Green Bay. But until Tex called me, I really had no intention of remaining in coaching much longer. If I'd been offered a head coaching job anywhere but Dallas, which is where I wanted to live, I wouldn't have taken it.

Coaching was only a six-month job in those days, and Landry earned just $12,000 a year with the Giants. A native of Mission, Texas, and a former University of Texas star, Landry had recently moved to Dallas and began selling insurance. When the AFL was getting organized in 1959, Landry fielded head coaching offers from Hunt in Dallas and Bud Adams in Houston. "Now, I didn't want Tom leaving the Giants, but I was even more concerned about the rival league getting him," Mara said. "So I phoned Tex Schramm and recommended they keep Tom in the NFL and hire him for their coach."

CBS sports chief Bill MacPhail recalled Schramm courting Landry even before Schramm gave notice that he was leaving the network. CBS bought tables at various banquets, and Schramm told his boss he wanted to invite Landry to one. "I couldn't figure that one out," MacPhail said. "Sure, Tom had gained a great reputation as coach of the Giants' defensive unit, but he wasn't exactly a well-known celebrity. I asked Tex why he wanted to bring Tom, and he said he just admired him. At the time, he was thinking about hiring Landry for his team in Dallas."

Landry was full of bright ideas, both as a player and as a coach.

He compensated for a lack of speed at cornerback by studying opposing offenses, which allowed him to usually line up in the right position. "When I came to the Giants [in 1954] as a defensive back, Tom would tell me what the offense was going to do on every play, and I would think there was no way he could know that," said Dick Nolan, who later became the San Francisco 49ers' head coach. "But finally I accepted it and trusted him, and he was nearly always right."

Though all teams studied game film of their opponents, Landry went the extra mile. He also compiled a list of an opponent's favorite plays in specific down-and-distance situations and then taught his defense to recognize those plays by identifying a formation or a player's movement. Recalled Hall of Fame middle linebacker Sam Huff:

> Tom Landry had a mind like a computer. He did tendencies of teams you were going to play. You knew [Cleveland's] Jim Brown was going to carry thirty or thirty-five times a game, so there was no need to look anywhere else.
>
> Plus, I knew where I was going to make the tackle as soon as I saw the back make his move because we played a team defense. The cornerback would come up and turn the ball inside. That's all he had to do. I used to make fifteen or twenty tackles a game.

That was the middle linebacker's role in the 4-3 defense, which Giants coach Steve Owen introduced in 1950 and Landry refined.

Owen used an "umbrella" defense, a 6-1 alignment that enhanced lateral pursuit against offenses attacking the edges. When Owens "flexed" his 6-1 defense, the ends dropped into zones and became outside linebackers. This move created a 4-3 defense, which also resulted when some teams, notably the Chicago Bears with Bill George in 1954, dropped the middle guard off a five-man line. No other pro defense has ever matched the staying power of the 4-3, which remains popular today.

With Landry running the Giants' defense and Lombardi the offense, Howell had an embarrassment of coaching riches. Joe King in the *New York World-Telegram* observed: "If the question is offense, Howell says, 'Ask Lombardi about that.' Defense? Tom Landry is the man to see. U.S. Steel does fairly well on that plan, but it is unorthodox in football and therefore suspect by some." A half century later, Howell's star assistants would have been designated as coordinators and earned more than $1 million a year.

Lombardi and Landry were fire and ice, as any television viewer could see when they became head coaches. Landry, a fighter pilot in World War II, was trim, poker-faced, and a devout Christian. He rarely swore. Lombardi was beefy and explosive and did not let his deep-seated Catholic faith tone down his salty vocabulary. When they coached in New York, Landry nicknamed Lombardi "Mr. High-Low" because of his moodiness. There was distance between them, especially when Lombardi had to listen to Yankee Stadium crowds chanting, "De-fense! De-fense!" The two would remain rivals into the dawn of the Super Bowl era.

"I would like to say I developed them [but] they had it when they came in," Howell told author Jim Terzian in *New York Giants.* "They did their jobs; you didn't have to keep after them. They were different as daylight and darkness, but they were great coaches and fine people." Had Mara been able to keep Landry or Lombardi as a head coach, the Giants might have dominated the NFL throughout the sixties and seventies. Instead, they hit hard times in the mid-1960s.

Lombardi's Packers won five NFL championships and two Super Bowls during the sixties. The Miami Dolphins, Pittsburgh Steelers, and Landry's Cowboys stood out in the seventies. Landry could not match Lombardi's fast start, however, because he took over a franchise that was fed mere scraps of talent. The 1960 NFL draft came and went in late November 1959 before Landry had a team, a handicap that would hurt him for years.

Murchison, a Dallas businessman, twice had failed to land an NFL franchise. He had asked Commissioner Bert Bell to let him buy the Dallas

Texans when they went broke in 1952. Bell refused because, according to Schramm, he wanted to put the team in Baltimore and deliver it to his friend Carroll Rosenbloom. More likely, Bell wanted to rid the NFL of a lawsuit the city of Baltimore filed after the Colts' dissolution in 1950. The team lasted just one season after being absorbed from the All-America Football Conference. Murchison had also tried to buy the San Francisco 49ers in 1954. He finally got a team when the NFL wanted to expand to Dallas and take on Hunt's Texans. Schramm, a University of Texas graduate, was intrigued by the prospect of running a pro franchise in Dallas.

"I kept hearing rumors about Dallas being awarded an expansion team, and that was what I really wanted," he said. "I mean, I wanted to start something from scratch and build it into a success." A mutual friend informed Murchison and Wynne that Schramm was interested in running their team. George Halas, the Chicago Bears' owner and driving force behind the NFL's expansion, told the Dallas partners that Schramm would be a good choice. In their first interview, Schramm warned Murchison to expect heavy financial losses for the first few years. He also said the franchise would not succeed if the owner meddled in football decisions. Murchison did not blink and hired Schramm for $36,500 a year, with options to buy 20 percent of the team's stock.

The Cowboys had to wait for the owners' meeting in January 1960 for admittance into the NFL, and Schramm could not afford to wait that long to start signing players. He suggested Murchison offer a personal services contract to Southern Methodist University's All-America quarterback "Dandy" Don Meredith. A local hero, Meredith would represent a prize catch for either Dallas franchise. "The feeling was, to win the battle of Dallas, you had to win the battle of Meredith," said Gil Brandt, the Cowboys' longtime director of player personnel.

Hunt, a former reserve end at SMU, knew all about Meredith's talent and drawing power. Hunt recalled,

I had seen every home game of his career, and he was

considered to be one of the top quarterbacks coming out of college football. For a team in Dallas, it would have been a very, very big thing to have his services. SMU was probably averaging 45,000 or 50,000 thousand a game, and our feeling was he would be very important to us.

Murchison and Hunt both made offers to Meredith even before either league held its 1960 draft. Meredith accepted Murchison's five-year, $150,000 contract, which was guaranteed even if the franchise did not materialize. Meredith told the *Kansas City Star* in 2000,

> My brother and I weren't sure if Murchison had $150,000. I had been accepted to law school and was excited about that and the idea they were going to pay me whether they got a franchise or not. They started talking about money, and I said, "Oh, really, all you want me to do is just play ball?"

Hunt, who was only six years older than the twenty-one-year-old Meredith, invited Meredith to his Dallas home to negotiate over barbecue. But when Hunt got ready to start his backyard grill, he realized he had no fluid. "We didn't have agents back then, it was just my brother and I," Meredith recalled. "So he had us down there picking up mimosa leaves to start his outdoor barbecue." Hunt told Meredith he would top Murchison's offer, but the details struck the quarterback as sketchy. "Lamar was new to all this," Meredith said. "He said, 'I'll give you $5,000 more.' My brother and I were on the way home, and we said, 'Did he mean $5,000 a year [more] or $155,000?' The negotiations were not terribly sophisticated."

Murchison signed Meredith and New Mexico running back Don Perkins to personal service contracts, and both players would eventually help the Cowboys grow into a playoff team. Meredith could not play for Murchison, though, if another NFL team drafted and signed him. So Halas drafted Meredith in the third round, with the understanding he would send him to Dallas if the team joined the league. Meanwhile, Hunt, hoping the NFL would turn down Dallas, made Meredith a territorial pick in the first AFL draft.

"It took a [near-]unanimous vote to expand and George Marshall, the owner of the Redskins and a cantankerous person, was determined there would be no expansion," Hunt recalled. "But the league was anxious to get a Dallas team started so we wouldn't get a running start." Marshall, indeed, voted against expansion, but Halas secured the 75 percent majority needed to award a franchise to Dallas for 1960 and to Minneapolis for 1961.

After the NFL draft, Schramm requested standard NFL player contracts so he could sign undrafted players, but Austin Gunsel, acting commissioner after Bell's death, would not permit Schramm to sign anyone until his franchise actually joined the league. Schramm, undeterred, counterfeited the official league contract and signed twenty-eight players anyway. "I had the contracts made up and then got in touch with [Rams owner] Dan Reeves," Schramm said. "I made a deal with Dan to pay the Rams $5,000 to let us use their information on players who were not drafted, the ones who would become free agents."

Schramm broke ground on a personnel department by hiring Brandt, who began scouting as a hobby while he attended the University of Wisconsin. He had made his living as a baby photographer before Schramm allowed him to fulfill his passion for scouting. Under the pretense of being a high school coach, Brandt convinced college coaches to send him game films. Elroy Hirsch, a boyhood neighbor in Milwaukee and later a star and executive with the Rams, helped Brandt land a part-time scouting job with that team. Brandt also scouted for the San Francisco 49ers.

The Dallas franchise's biggest hurdle—acceptance by the league—was yet to come. Murchison, Wynne, and Schramm anxiously waited a week in Miami Beach before the expansion vote. NFL owners first struggled for twenty-three ballots before electing Pete Rozelle as commissioner. Beyond voting in the Dallas partners, NFL owners did them no favors. The player allocation format doomed the new team to a bleak start. Each of twelve teams could protect twenty-five of thirty-six players on their rosters. From a pool of 132, the Cowboys could pick thirty-six players, though no more than three from one team.

"The NFL gave us the pleasure of selecting three of the worst football players off each team in the league," Landry said, "refused to give us a draft and then said, 'O.K., boys, let's play.'" He later reflected that "it wasn't an intelligent decision" to take over a team under such circumstances.

Halas, as promised, delivered Meredith—but for a price. "Halas's idea was to draft him to protect him from somebody else doing it," Schramm said. "Sounds great. When the draft was over, he said, 'How many draft choices are you going to give me for Meredith?'" Schramm sent the Bears a third-round pick in 1962.

Meredith rode the bench while Eddie LeBaron, who stood somewhere around five feet eight inches tall, started for an 0–11–1 team in 1960. "Our guys were afraid to touch the football, it was so dangerous," Landry recalled. "Eddie LeBaron used to raise his hand for a fair catch before taking the snap from center." There was no sense throwing the rookie quarterback to the wolves. "LeBaron and I used to joke I was bigger than the left guard and I could outrun the halfback," Meredith said. There was nothing humorous, though, about the punishment he absorbed behind a weak line. Meredith suffered a shoulder separation in 1961; a hand injury in 1962; knee, ankle, and shoulder problems in 1964; an arm injury in 1965; and bruised ribs and a broken nose that forced him to play with a protective mask in 1966.

The Dallas team at first was called the Steers and then the Rangers. The Rangers were a minor-league baseball team expected to fold, but they hung on for the 1960 season. To avoid confusion, the NFL team became the Cowboys.

The Cowboys got off to a 3–1 start in 1961 but finished 4–9–1. "The world doesn't stop when you lose," Landry said. "You must think about the good things that happened to you. You must look ahead. The only way a person can become strong is to have setbacks." Beneath the surface, Schramm, Landry, and Brandt were assembling an organization that would boast twenty straight winning seasons, five NFC championships, and two Super Bowl victories.

At the start, however, the Cowboys practiced in a minor-league baseball stadium and used a ladies' restroom as their training room. Their front office and coaching staff shared one room in the Automobile Club Building. The Texans had their own practice field and offices in the Mercantile Securities Building. They also had first pick of Cotton Bowl dates, which forced the Cowboys to play their first two home games on a Saturday and a Friday night. This schedule enraged college and high school supporters, who accused the new NFL team of poaching their traditional game days. The Cowboys announced a home crowd of 30,000 for their opener, a 35–28 loss to the Pittsburgh Steelers on September 24, while the Texans played their first home game September 25 and claimed a crowd of 42,000 for a 17–0 victory over the Los Angeles Chargers.

Hunt was a gung ho promoter. One of his pet promotions was Friend of the Barber Day, which offered a free upper deck seat to anyone wearing a barber's smock. He started the Huddle Club, which for one dollar gave a kid free admission to all home games and a Texans T-shirt. Hunt devised numerous giveaways and organized a season ticket drive. "He tried every kind of promotion you ever heard of," recalled Hunt's widow, Norma. "That Barnum and Bailey side of Lamar was amazing. He loved that part of the business."

A high school history teacher in suburban Richardson, Norma Knobel met Lamar Hunt when she was recruited to help sell Texans tickets. She and the other volunteers attended training classes, which Hunt sometimes observed, and a convertible was promised to the top salesperson. Norma Hunt recalls that she was beaten out for the car when a rival swooped in just before the deadline with a large corporate order. "But no amount of spreading the word did any good," she recalled. "The crowds were so small!"

For the Texans' second home game, October 2 against the New York Titans, Hunt held a Texans' Teen Salute, which offered free admission to any student with a ticket stub from a high school game the previous Friday night. Schramm considered this promotion a ploy to remind fans that the Cowboys had just competed with the high schools on a Friday night and drew an estimated crowd of only 18,500 for a 27–25 loss to the Philadelphia Eagles. Schramm said,

> People got so angry that they even turned on Roy Rogers, King of the Cowboys. We brought him in for our first game and had him ride in a car around the Cotton Bowl. Fans started throwing ice at him, and we had to get him out of there. I'm surprised Lamar Hunt didn't have a day where ice throwers at our games got in free to see the Texans.

While the Cowboys went winless in 1960, the Texans finished 8-6 and were led by Abner Haynes, a running back from North Texas State. Both teams, however, began losing millions. "At first Hunt proposed to play us in a 'loser leave town' game, but we refused," Schramm said in Bob St. John's book *Tex!* "Then the joke going around town a year or so later was that the two teams should play and the loser had to *stay* in town."

When the Cowboys announced they would charge $3.90 for reserved seats, which was standard for college games in Texas, Hunt priced his reserved seats at $4.00 to imply his product was superior. Schramm said in Jeff Miller's *Going Long,*

> The bad thing about having two teams in one city is not the actual competition. It's the fact that it totally separates your city. I'm sure that both teams feel the same thing in New York. When I was with the Rams, for several years there was a new league at that time, too. I learned then of the problems in a two-team city. And the biggest example was at the newspapers. In

Dallas, we had writers there that were Cowboys writers, and
we had writers that were Texans writers. And they weren't
friendly.

Yet the players on both teams did not necessarily exchange
animosity. "I had no basic conception of the Cowboys," said Texans
running back Curtis McClinton, the AFL Rookie of the Year in 1962. "I
knew they existed, but I never interfaced with any of their players."

According to Schramm, Hunt met with him and Murchison after
the Texans won the AFL championship in 1962 and indicated he might
move. According to Texans publicist Bob Halford,

We knew both teams weren't going to exist in Dallas. And
there was a good chance that the first team that got a good
opportunity to go somewhere else would take it. I don't know
if the Cowboys would have left or not. But if we hadn't left,
I don't think that Murchison would have kept ownership of
the team because his money was getting short at the time. His
pockets weren't as deep as Lamar's.

Hunt was persuaded to move to Kansas City in 1963 by its mayor,
H. Roe Bartle, nicknamed "the Chief." Partly to honor the mayor, the
team was renamed the "Chiefs."

The Chiefs were not well supported until 1966, when they won
the AFL championship and finally won over the town. Dallas, however,
turned into a gold mine for the Cowboys. Murchison paid a $50,000
franchise fee and $500,000 for the rights to draft veteran players. In
September 2007, *Forbes* magazine valued the Cowboys at $1.5 billion
and called the team "the world's most valuable sports franchise." Who
could have foreseen this destiny in the early 1960s?

Even with the Texans gone, the Cowboys' home crowds in 1963
topped 30,000 fans just once. They finished 4–10, giving Landry a four-
year record of 13–38–3. With fans screaming for Landry's firing and

with many players fed up with his cold and overbearing style, Schramm worried that his coach was being undermined. Convinced that Landry was on the right track, Schramm advised Murchison to stay the course. The owner shocked the city of Dallas on February 5, 1964, by giving Landry a new ten-year contract. The coach needed more than job security, however; he needed better talent. Schramm sought to build a scouting system second to none.

During his decade with the Rams, Schramm learned at the foot of Reeves, an owner who also was a pioneer in scouting and draft preparation. In Dallas, Schramm would refine the principles he learned from Reeves and make good use of a new and powerful tool. While working for CBS at the 1960 Winter Olympics at Squaw Valley, California, Schramm became fascinated with IBM computers. They could digest a flood of statistics from Olympic events and quickly sort them into official results and medal standings. Schramm asked IBM engineers if their computers could process scouting reports to rate football prospects. He was told that the computers just needed the relevant information.

Once Schramm took over in Dallas, he phoned his IBM contacts and sought their help in using computers for talent evaluation. He was referred to Salam Qureishi, a programming expert in Palo Alto, California. Qureishi was from India, knew nothing about football, and at first struggled to communicate with Schramm. Still Schramm forged ahead. First, he had to identify qualities critical to evaluating an NFL prospect that went beyond such easily measurable credentials as height, weight, and forty-yard dash times. He picked five variables: character, quickness and body control, competitiveness, mental alertness, and strength and explosion.

Next, Schramm needed specific language that would keep college coaches and the Cowboys' scouts all using the same variables when rating prospects. The computer had no use for common scouting clichés. So the Cowboys devised fifteen statements to evaluate personal characteristics, physical qualities, and position skills. Each statement would be graded from one to nine, with a nine meaning a statement exactly described the player.

Though Schramm would have preferred keeping this project to himself, it was too expensive for one franchise to develop. He invited the Rams and 49ers to join the Cowboys, and each contributed more than $300,000 over the next four years. They called themselves "Troika," the first of the scouting combines that would expand into league-wide institutions. The Cowboys' first computer printout was produced for the 1965 draft, which was held November 28, 1964. Alas, the computer produced no magic. The Cowboys, drafting sixth, had a productive but not sensational draft. They picked quarterback Craig Morton, who would lead them to one Super Bowl, in the first round; Malcolm Walker, a two-year starting center, in the second round; and Jethro Pugh, who would become a fixture at defensive tackle, in the eleventh round.

The Cowboys had actually fared better the year before, when inside information and a few gambles brought them safety Mel Renfro and quarterback Roger Staubach, both future Hall of Fame players, and Bob Hayes, a game-breaking wide receiver. Renfro, from Oregon, scared off some teams because he had been stabbed in the wrist during an argument with his wife, but the Cowboys knew Renfro would fully recover and drafted him in the second round. He made the Pro Bowl in each of his first ten seasons. Hayes, a receiver at Florida A&M who would catch seventy-one touchdown passes for the Cowboys, lasted until the seventh round because he was best known as a world-class sprinter. Schramm had a weakness for speed, and multisport athletes intrigued Brandt. They picked Hayes and Staubach after Landry left to prepare for his next opponent.

Staubach represented the Cowboys' biggest coup of the 1964 draft or, for that matter, any draft. He was a junior at Annapolis and the only uniform he would wear for the next five years belonged to the U.S. Navy. Schramm and Brandt drafted him as a "future" pick, who could not be signed for another year, but then he would start his four-year hitch. A familiar rival, the Chiefs, also made Staubach a future pick in the AFL draft. Staubach explained he wanted to play in the more established league and signed with the Cowboys after the 1964 Army-Navy game. He joined the team in 1969, became the starter midway through the 1971 season, and led the Cowboys to a 24–3 victory over the Dolphins in the first of his four Super Bowl appearances.

The Cowboys kept refining their scouting and consistently improved through the draft. They hit the jackpot in 1975, when they drafted the "Dirty Dozen," all of whom made the roster and helped the Cowboys rebound from an 8–6 season and win the NFC title. The Cowboys' computer also helped target such undrafted players as wide receiver Drew Pearson, safety Cliff Harris, and cornerback Everson Walls. They totaled thirteen Pro Bowl berths for the Cowboys.

The Cowboys' painstaking franchise building finally began paying off in 1966. They finished 10–3–1, and Landry was named NFL Coach of the Year. In the league championship game, Landry butted heads with a familiar rival—Lombardi. Landry's old colleague already had three NFL titles under his belt and had transformed the Packers into the NFL's dominant team. The Cowboys, meanwhile, were entering their phase as "Next Year's Champion."

In the 1966 NFL title game in Dallas, the Packers, behind Bart Starr's four touchdown passes, led the Cowboys 34–20. Meredith and wide receiver Frank Clarke then hooked up on a sixty-eight-yard touchdown pass, and the Cowboys got the ball back with a chance to tie near the end of the game. They had a first down at the Green Bay two-yard line after safety Tom Brown was called for pass interference on Clarke. On fourth down from the two, Meredith rolled to his right and was pressured by blitzing linebacker Dave Robinson. He threw a desperation pass for Hayes, but Brown intercepted it.

Landry and Lombardi met again in the 1967 NFL championship game, better known as the "Ice Bowl" because the temperature at kickoff in Green Bay was thirteen degrees below zero, with the wind chill measured at minus forty-six degrees. The Cowboys led 17-14 in the final minute before Starr scored on his famous one-yard sneak. The Packers used their last timeout with sixteen seconds left and probably would not have had enough time to kick a field goal had Starr been stopped. But a double-team block on the Cowboys' Pugh gave Starr the hole he needed. The loss was especially bitter for Meredith, who had endured so much criticism and punishment while falling short of a championship. "It's most disappointing to have that happen twice in a row," he said. "I guess we can do everything but win the big one."

Meredith returned for the 1968 season, which ended with a 31–20 playoff loss to the Cleveland Browns. Landry replaced him with Morton during that game, and Meredith's rocky relationship with Landry reached an all-time low. Meredith longed to call his own plays, as was common in that era, but Landry sent in a play on every down. "Tom, I don't want to talk to you," Meredith told his coach the night before a game. "Just slip your game plan under the door."

Landry was involved in both offense and defense, though most NFL head coaches focus on no more than one area. Although he came up through the ranks as a defensive player and an assistant, he developed the league's flashiest offense. The Cowboys' attack featured multiple sets, shifting, and a shotgun formation.

Meredith, only thirty-one years old, retired after the 1968 season and seamlessly switched to a career as an actor and broadcaster, hitting his stride as a *Monday Night Football* analyst who sparred on the air with Howard Cosell. "I begged him not to retire," Schramm said. "The next year, I tried to get him to come back. The sad thing about it is, he would have been a Hall of Fame quarterback."

The year after Meredith retired, the Browns again knocked the Cowboys out of the playoffs. "[They] were the most miserable, toughest coaching years I had," Landry said. "When you take a good team demoralized by defeat in big games and have to turn them around, it's the toughest coaching job you can face."

The Cowboys finally reached the Super Bowl in January 1971, only to lose another big game. Colts linebacker Mike Curtis made a late interception of a Morton pass and helped set up a thirty-two-yard field goal by Jim O'Brien that broke a 13–13 tie with five seconds left. Defensive tackle Bob Lilly heaved his helmet down the field in frustration. But a year later, the Cowboys finally won the big one, defeating the Dolphins 24–3. "I don't think I'm really conscious of my feelings yet," Landry said. "This is certainly my biggest thrill."

Fans throughout Dallas and the nation excused the Cowboys' heartbreaking losses and embraced them as they played in three more Super Bowls during the 1970s. Landry, Brandt, and Schramm kept the Dallas machine humming. When the players who brought the Cowboys their first wave of success began to retire, their brain trust built another Super Bowl championship team, in 1977, with an almost entirely different roster.

Landry, Brandt, and Schramm sustained their success to the mid-1980s. Murchison's health was failing in 1983, and he asked Schramm to find a buyer. The Cowboys were sold in early 1984 for $60 million to an eleven-member limited partnership headed by Dallas businessman H. R. (Bum) Bright. The new owners, however, bought the Cowboys on the way down. The team enjoyed its twentieth straight winning season in 1985, but it had losing seasons each of the next two years and fell to 3–13 in 1988. Attendance was declining, too.

Landry refused to throw in the towel. He said in mid-February 1989 that he planned to coach into the next decade and make the Cowboys a winner again. He never got that chance. Bright sold the team for $140 million on February 25, 1989, to Arkansas businessman Jerry Jones. The new owner made it obvious he would replace Landry with Jimmy Johnson, a former college teammate who had coached a powerhouse at the University of Miami. Schramm convinced Jones to pay his respects to Landry and fire him in person at his Austin home.

When NFL owners approved the sale of the Cowboys on April 18, 1989, Schramm resigned and became president of the World League of American Football, the NFL's now defunct developmental league. Brandt was kept on board through the April 23 draft, in which Johnson laid the foundation for three Super Bowl victories by taking UCLA quarterback Troy Aikman with the first overall pick. Brandt was fired shortly thereafter.

Jones's clumsy firing of Landry and scene-stealing entrance upset many fans and media critics. He upset Schramm, too. "You could tell right from the beginning that he didn't give a damn about history," Schramm told Jim Dent in a 1995 Jones biography. "You can tell this man has absolutely no feeling for the past. You almost expected him to take the stars off the helmets."

Landry was inducted into the Pro Football Hall of Fame in 1990 and died ten years later at age seventy-five. Schramm was inducted a year later on the strength of his success with the Cowboys, his role in negotiating the AFL-NFL merger, and his twenty-three-year stint on the NFL Competition Committee. He died in 2003 at age eighty-three. After his firing, Landry did not return to Texas Stadium for a game until 1993, when he was invited to see his name added to the Cowboys' Ring of Honor.

Johnson took that occasion to pay tribute to the three who built a football team from scratch. "That's one reason why the Dallas Cowboys, in a lot of people's minds, are special, and that's one of the reasons I wanted to coach the Dallas Cowboys," Johnson said. "Tom Landry, Tex Schramm, Gil Brandt—I think they were ahead of a lot of the league for a long period of time."

They were among the most notable movers and shakers in pro football during 1959, an unforgettable year of blossoming for the sport. The Cowboys were born, and in that year an entire new league was formed. And the leader who brought the game to the brink of a fabulous future unexpectedly died.

5

Last of His Kind

Bert Bell recognized pro football's defining moment as soon as he saw it. Bell sat in his commissioner's box at Yankee Stadium as he watched Baltimore Colts fullback Alan Ameche plunge into the end zone and climax a remarkable NFL championship game. A packed stadium and a television audience of fifty million, including President Dwight Eisenhower at his Gettysburg, Pennsylvania farm, viewed the Colts' 23–17 victory over the New York Giants in sudden-death overtime. "This is the greatest day in the history of pro football!" Bell shouted.

Bell, the NFL's commissioner since 1946, did not have to wait to read the show's reviews to appreciate its ramifications. "He had tears in his eyes," recalled his son Upton Bell. "I think he knew that everything he worked so hard for . . . I think he knew before all the people who have written about it since then . . . he knew that pro football had arrived that day."

As NFL commissioner, Bell championed revenue sharing and competitive balance. He brought the league into the television age and forcefully dealt with a gambling scandal early in his administration. He guided the NFL through a bitter and costly battle with an upstart league. This praise could pass for a eulogy of Pete Rozelle's, and it's a cruel trick of history that Bell is a foggy memory while Rozelle is celebrated as the most famous sports commissioner of them all.

Bell's life had a huge impact on professional football. So did his death on October 11, 1959. The NFL was desperate for a strong hand when Bell was asked to guide the fragile league in the postwar era. Upton Bell, former general manager of the New England Patriots, said,

> I honestly believe that if he had not come along, the game would not have been saved. He came along at a crucial time. Nobody had as much influence on a sport as Bert Bell had at that time. He was featured on the cover of the *Saturday Evening Post*. Has there ever been a sport that had a unique character who was a coach, owner and commissioner? It never happened before, and it never will happen again.

Nor will the NFL ever have another commissioner saddled with so many responsibilities. A small army at NFL headquarters today is needed to handle all the issues Bell was forced to juggle. Owners routinely dumped the thorniest problems in his lap. "They became so reliant on him doing everything," said Upton Bell. "He took care of the schedule, the pension, the television networks. They did nothing. He had done so well that when a difficult issue came up, the owners would say, 'You know what? We're not going to table this. Bert, you do it.'"

Bell, sixty-four, undoubtedly would have picked a later time to die, but he may not have picked another place. He died at Franklin Field during a game between the Philadelphia Eagles and the Pittsburgh Steelers, both of which Bell had once owned. The stadium was also home to the University of Pennsylvania when Bell, the captain and quarterback, led the 1916 Quakers to the Rose Bowl.

Upton Bell, in a *Boston Globe* retrospective, recalled his father's Sunday ritual when the Eagles played at home. Bert Bell would put on a brown suit, have breakfast, and attend church. Before the game, he would visit the Eagles' offices, drink coffee, and chat with team president Joe (Jiggs) Donoghue. Before the last game Bell would ever watch, his son recalls him slipping some cash to John (Bull) Lipski, one of Bell's old Eagles players who was down on his luck.

Upton Bell also asked the commissioner for some cash. It seems he needed more tickets for his friends and money for a bite after the game. The younger Bell recalled his father teasing him and yelling to Donoghue in his gravelly voice, "I need three more tickets and Upton will be out to pay for them." Bell, as commissioner, had a free box on the fifty-yard line, yet he insisted on buying his own tickets.

Upton Bell said,

> He was the only commissioner who ever paid for his own tickets. He wanted to make decisions based on not owing anything to anybody. He never sat in the commissioner's box. I sat there, next to the visiting owners. I knew what was going on with them as much as he did. He was in the press box, the end zone, all over the stadium. He talked to the fans. I wasn't surprised that's where he was when he died.

Before he began roaming the stadium, however, Bell would instruct his son and friends on how to behave in the commissioner's box. "First, don't root outwardly," Upton Bell recalled. "As the son of the commissioner, we're expected to be neutral. Second, smile. If you're talking to the relatives of visiting team owners, compliment their team lavishly, no matter how lousy they're playing."

On that fateful day, the Steelers were led by future Hall of Fame quarterback Bobby Layne, who ran for a touchdown, threw two touchdown passes, and kicked a field goal and three extra points. But the Eagles' defensive front harassed Layne all day and prevented him from throwing deep. An eighteen-yard touchdown pass from Norm Van Brocklin to Tommy McDonald gave the Eagles a 28–24 victory.

Late in the fourth quarter, as the Steelers threatened to take the lead, Upton Bell noticed fans high in a corner of the end zone bent over someone sprawled in the stands and wearing a brown suit. He assumed someone had passed out because of the unseasonably warm weather. Then he saw an oxygen tank being carried up the stadium steps. Until he borrowed a pair of binoculars, it did not occur to Upton Bell that the man needing help might be his father. He remembered,

> Another look, it's my father. He's motionless. I jump the railing and start to run across the field. People are screaming, "It's Bert Bell!" For some reason, I'm out of breath after my first few steps. He seems so far away, like a mirage that keeps receding before me. But his face is now covered when I arrive. I ask someone how he's doing. No one answers. The scene is swimming all around me. Somebody's screaming that the damn oxygen tank won't work . . . and to think we got it from the Steelers. "You mean," I ask dumbly, "the Steelers' oxygen tank doesn't work!"
>
> The ambulance ride was quick, and his hands were cold. When we got to the hospital, they wheeled him into the waiting room. Everything was noise and confusion. Flash bulbs were popping and newspeople were everywhere. A priest was talking quietly in Latin. A reporter was asking for the names and ages of the children. "It's not over yet," I told him, but now my father's hand felt like a rock and his face seemed etched in stone. Other people were asking questions and shedding tears as I left the waiting room and struggled to my car. It had been a scene with no redeeming qualities. My father, a public man, hadn't been allowed to die alone, and that was that.

The NFL, under Bell, had made great strides. Yet, it seemed uncertain what to do next. The NFL was stuck on twelve teams, and its only significant post-Depression expansion was the 1950 addition of three franchises from the failed All-America Football Conference. Bell was loath to expand until the weaker franchises stabilized. The Eagles and Chicago Cardinals each had won two games in 1958 and the Green Bay Packers only one. "What my father insisted upon was, 'Until every team is in the black, we're not going to expand anywhere,'" Upton Bell said. "They had to get their own house in order. There were still teams not making money."

Several NFL owners discouraged expansion because it would force them to divide the pie into more slices. Texas oilman Bud Adams learned that in the spring of 1958 when he lobbied Ed Pauley, part owner of the Los Angeles Rams, for an NFL team in Houston. "He told me the NFL was not going to expand," Adams recalled. "[He said,] 'Some of those guys, that's their livelihood. They don't have an oil company like you do. They need all the revenues they can get on the front end and not be dividing it up.'"

There also was the Chicago problem. The city was populous enough for two well-run franchises but housed one perennial power, the Bears, and one perennial doormat, the Cardinals. Walter Wolfner and his wife, Violet, owned the latter. Bears owner George Halas, wishing the Cardinals would get out of his hair and his television market, offered the Wolfners as much as $500,000 if they would move to another city. The Wolfners were not committed to staying yet not ready to move, and they opposed expansion. They were holding up progress, but other owners did not force their hand. The league was too clubby for its own good.

"We owners were a tight little group," Halas acknowledged.

> As with most organizations, we perhaps were too unresponsive to newcomers wanting to join our league. After almost a quarter of a century, professional football [in the mid-1940s] was confined to ten cities. Several other cities were big enough to support a professional team. College football was strong from coast to coast. But we liked things the way they were. We did our best to keep things that way. Looking back, I can see how our closed door policy was certain sooner or later to produce trouble for us.

The All-America Football Conference, an upstart with several well-armed owners, took on the NFL in 1946, but four years later it waved a white flag. So when Lamar Hunt and the AFL came along in 1959, Halas was confident he could put the newcomers in the same graveyard as the AAFC. Despite protecting his owners' interests, Bell seemed less hostile to the new league than most of his owners, and it is a point of conjecture whether the leagues might have merged with less acrimony had Bell lived longer.

Bell was a tireless lobbyist in Washington, D.C., promoting issues important to the NFL. He envied the antitrust exemption Major League Baseball enjoyed, though the U.S. Supreme Court decision in 1922 that had established that exemption was considered badly flawed. Bell tried to make his case for an exemption when he testified in front of the U.S. Senate Judiciary Committee's Sub-Committee on Anti-Trust Monopoly in late July 1959. He stayed in touch with Hunt and received his permission to reveal the formation of the AFL during his testimony. That news would allow Bell to convey the false impression that NFL owners welcomed competition. He claimed the NFL's rivalry with the AAFC had been "a great thing for pro football" because of the public debate over which league was strongest. Reminded that the NFL did not exactly welcome the AAFC, Bell replied, "I know, but I can't help what the owners think. I know what it did. I will tell you, [the AFL] is great and I have talked it over with every owner and not one of them has an objection to it, not one of them."

Bell did not get the antitrust exemption, but his testimony reinforced his knack for giving the league a respected public face. He exuded both substance and style, and it's not surprising that NFL owners considered Bell irreplaceable. "His death is a tragic thing," said Edwin J. Anderson, president and general manager of the Detroit Lions. "Bell has done more for professional football than any other man. He will be sorely missed by the entire league."

The San Francisco 49ers' Vic Morabito, an original AAFC owner, said, "We lost our strongest member. He truly cannot be replaced. He was devoted to the entire league twenty-four hours a day. He loved us all and we loved him."

Washington Redskins owner George Preston Marshall, not noted for speaking kindly of anyone else in the league, said, "They will never find a commissioner as good as Bell, no matter whom they pick."

Added New York Giants president Jack Mara: "To us on the Giants and to the rest of the league, Bert Bell was the league. We all looked on Bert Bell as indispensable. I'm too shocked to even think about who should be his successor." This sentiment was not merely a case of speaking well of the dead. NFL owners respected Bell's leadership through several crises. They had asked him to take over in 1946 from Elmer Layden, the commissioner since 1941. Before Layden, the NFL had been led by a series of presidents who lacked the authority to govern effectively.

The NFL commissioners' résumés reveal much about the league's evolution. Layden, one of Notre Dame's Four Horsemen in 1924, was hired with the hope that he could bring college football's glamour and popularity to the NFL. He could not. "No owner has made money from pro football but a lot have gone broke thinking they could," NFL president Joe Carr said in 1939.

Bell was a triple threat. He had been a college star and both a head coach and an owner in the NFL. Rozelle was the first NFL commissioner who had not played the game, yet others still considered him a "football man" because of his record as a general manager of the Los Angeles Rams. The job's qualifications continued to tilt more toward business and less toward football. When Jim Finks, a well-liked and well-respected general manager, threw his hat in the ring to succeed Rozelle, he lost out to Paul Tagliabue, a league lawyer, in 1989. Tagliabue's successor, Roger Goodell, took over in 2006 after serving as the NFL's chief operating officer. He had impressed owners with his creativity in the financing and construction of NFL stadiums in the face of diminished public funding. He is, however, a far cry from Bert Bell.

As a commissioner, Bell was the last of a breed. In his book *Halas*, Halas, one of Bell's best friends, described him like this:

> Bert was different from most of us. He was high society. His mother was named Fleurette. His father had Cromwell for a middle name. Bert was christened DeBenneville. A brother was governor of the state, his father attorney general for the state and his grandfather a congressman. Of course the family was rich. Bert had, in turn, a nanny, a pony, a Marmon sportster. His mother died when he was seventeen. His father spoiled him expertly. Bert was thrown out of three prep schools.

DeBenneville was a name from Bell's mother's side of the family. "If you don't think I had to fight to get people to call me 'Bert,' then I must have dreamed all those playground battles," he said. When Bell became a football star at Haverford School outside Philadelphia, John Cromwell Bell was asked if his son might play college football out of state. "He'll go to Penn or he'll go to hell," the attorney general of Pennsylvania replied.

Bell was a free-spending bon vivant during the 1920s and also served as an assistant coach at Penn. He eventually went to work for his father, managing a luxury hotel, and met the love of his life. "The stock market crash eliminated his fortune," Halas wrote. "He continued to be a heller, but on a reduced scale. In 1932 he fell for a Ziegfeld Follies girl, Frances Upton. He wanted to marry her. 'It's alcohol or me,' she said. He finished his glass, turned it upside down and never again drank anything stronger than coffee."

Bell and Frances Upton were already engaged when he bought the defunct Frankford Yellow Jackets. They were based in a northeast Philadelphia suburb and won more games than any other NFL team from 1924 through 1929. They finished last in 1931 and went bankrupt during that season. Bell borrowed $2,500 from his fiancée, who was then a musical comedy actress, and, with former Penn teammate Lud Wray, organized a group to buy the Yellow Jackets franchise in 1933. They named the new team the Eagles after the blue eagle that symbolized the National Recovery Administration, which was set up to encourage fair competition among business owners and establish fair wage and hour guidelines for workers.

Wray was the Eagles' first coach and guided them to a 9–21–1 record in three years before the franchise went bust. Bell bought the team out of bankruptcy for $4,500 and became his own coach, going 10–44–2 from 1936 to 1940. During a loss to the Bears, Bell became enraged because Chicago's Luke Johnsos tricked an Eagle into flipping him a lateral and then ran with the ball past the Eagles' bench. Bell ran down the sideline, step for step with Johnsos, and berated him all the way. Although Bell stood only five feet eight inches tall, in later years he weighed 220 pounds.

Bell learned the hard way that the NFL was divided among the haves and have-nots. The Green Bay Packers, Chicago Bears, and New York Giants usually sat at or near the top of the league in the early 1930s and were the only teams with healthy bottom lines. "We three drew the biggest crowds," Halas wrote. "We had the most money. We could pay more for players. Good college players wanted to join our winning clubs. The prospect was that each year the strong would become stronger, the weak weaker."

At the league meeting in the spring of 1935, Bell proposed that the NFL adopt a college draft. He suggested that each team submit a list of top college players, who would then be placed in a common pool. Teams would draft players in inverse order of the previous season's standings. The Eagles, which finished 2–9 in 1935, would draft first. If a team and player could not agree on contract terms, the league president would arbitrate. If that process failed, the team that drafted the player was obliged to trade him. The unsigned player also had the option of sitting out a year and negotiating as a free agent. Any player not drafted would also be a free agent. The basics of Bell's draft have remained in place for more than seventy years.

But the draft did not prove much help to the Eagles. Their first pick in the inaugural 1936 draft was University of Chicago halfback Jay Berwanger, the first winner of what would be called the Heisman Trophy. Berwanger did not play professionally, and the Eagles could not sign any of their nine picks. They finished 1–11 in 1936 and in Bell's five seasons as coach won more than two games only once.

Bell ended up creating what is now the most popular off-the-field event in professional sports. Not even Rozelle, the master of public relations, seriously considered ESPN's first offer to televise the draft. Bell's proposal for a draft passed unanimously. Halas said,

> Of course, some people saw in the draft an aspect of selfishness on the part of the owners. They claimed we were trying to hold down salaries by reducing the negotiating rights of the best players. There is some truth in this argument. But time proved that by leveling the clubs, the draft system heightened the attractiveness of the sport. It created bigger audiences, which brought bigger revenues, which brought higher salaries of all players.

The Eagles kept bleeding red ink, and Bell no longer could afford to operate the team after the 1940 season. He remained an NFL owner only because Steelers owner Art Rooney engineered a complicated transaction that saw them become co-owners of the Pittsburgh franchise. On December 9, 1940, Rooney sold the Steelers to Alexis Thompson of New York, a thirty-year-old heir to a $6 million fortune in steel stocks. Rooney then bought a half interest in the Eagles from Bell. Rooney and Bell then traded franchises with Thompson, and each took players from both rosters. Rooney and Bell moved the Eagles to Pittsburgh and renamed them the "Steelers" while Thompson took the Steelers to Philadelphia and renamed them the "Eagles."

Bell was head coach and Rooney general manager of the Steelers, which lost their first two games in 1941. Bell asked Rooney if he had any ideas to improve the team. "Bert," Rooney replied, "did you ever think about changing coaches?"

Aldo (Buff) Donelli and then Walt Kiesling led the Steelers through a 1-9-1 finish. Then Bell finally hit the jackpot in the first round of the 1942 draft. Bill Dudley, a halfback from Virginia, led the NFL in rushing as a rookie and helped the Steelers finish 7–4, their first winning record since they were founded as the Pirates in 1933. However, Dudley, went into military service the next season, and the Steelers could not have survived the war without a couple of mergers. They combined their war-depleted roster with that of the Eagles in 1943 and became the Phil-Pitt Steagles. They combined with the Chicago Cardinals in 1944 and became Card-Pitt.

NFL owners wanted fresh leadership after the war, especially with competition on the horizon. Arch Ward, sports editor of the *Chicago Tribune* and founder of the annual College All-Star Game at Soldier Field, began organizing a new league late in 1944. He was motivated, as Hunt would be fifteen years later, by the NFL's reluctance to expand. Ward asked Halas to help his friend, actor Don Ameche, get a franchise in Buffalo, which would later be moved to Los Angeles. Halas explained he had promised the Cardinals first crack at a West Coast franchise. NFL owners voted down the Buffalo proposal, and Ward recruited owners for the AAFC.

NFL owners wanted a commissioner knowledgeable enough to run their league and feisty enough to subdue the new league. Bell seemed the obvious candidate. He replaced Layden on January 11, 1946, and received a three-year contract at $20,000 a year. He sold his share of the Steelers to Rooney and moved the league office from Chicago to Philadelphia. "If you wanted to see the commissioner, you'd have to go to Philly because that was his city and he'd never leave," recalled CBS director of sports Bill MacPhail. Bell operated with a skeleton staff in Center City Philadelphia and later moved the office to nearby Bala Cynwyd. He worked on some of his most important projects, like the league schedule, at his kitchen table in suburban Narberth.

Bell's first year as commissioner was momentous. The NFL became national in scope when Cleveland Rams owner Dan Reeves received permission to move his team, the defending league champion, to Los Angeles. The Rams signed Kenny Washington and Woody Strode, the first African American players of the NFL's modern era. Postwar prosperity brought the NFL record attendance, about thirty-one thousand fans per game in 1946, and Bell promoted his league's popularity by presenting a gold-plated lifetime pass to President Harry Truman.

But the AAFC signed more than its fair share of top college players, and the competition pinched teams in both leagues. Bell's biggest headache, however, was the revelation that gamblers had tried to fix the 1946 NFL championship game between the Giants and the Bears on December 15 at the Polo Grounds. Rumors of a fix led to a New York Police Department investigation, and the night before the game, Mayor William O'Dwyer phoned Bell to tell him that he and the police had interrogated Giants running back Merle Hapes and quarterback Frank Filchock. Hapes admitted to turning down a bribe from Alvin Paris, a twenty-eight-year-old gambler, while Filchock pleaded ignorance.

Bell suspended Hapes but allowed Filchock to play, and despite suffering a broken nose, he threw touchdowns passes, along with six interceptions, in the Bears' 24–14 victory. Filchock finally admitted that he, too, had been offered a bribe, and Bell suspended both indefinitely. Upon announcing the suspensions, Bell said, "Professional football cannot continue to exist unless it is based on absolute honesty. The players must be not only absolutely honest; they must be above suspicion."

Filchock was reinstated in 1950 and Hapes in 1954, though their NFL careers essentially were finished. Realizing that insider information obtained by gamblers could undermine the league's integrity, Bell announced that, starting in 1947, the NFL would list injured players and their likely status for upcoming games. Weekly injury lists still are issued today.

Though "parity" became a well-worn word during the Rozelle era, it was Bell who pushed his owners to enhance the league's competitive balance. "On any given Sunday, any team in our league can beat any other team," Bell loved to say. Though that assertion was often not the case, he knew that arranging the league schedule was the best way to level the playing field. When Bell took office, each owner selfishly wanted a schedule that would bring him the most revenue. Because the home team earned 60 percent of the gate after stadium expenses, most owners angled for home games against such popular draws as the Giants and the Bears. After that, they wanted opponents they could beat.

"Weak teams should play other weak teams while the strong teams are playing other strong teams early in the year," Bell said. Long before the league had a scheduling department and computer programs, each off-season Bell came up with a schedule aimed at competitive balance. Upton Bell remembers his father coming home excitedly from an Eagles game and shouting to his wife, "Guess what? It's week four, and they're all still in the race."

Competitive balance helped explain the NFL's conquest of the AAFC. The four-year war cost both leagues about $6 million, but the NFL was better equipped to stand the losses. Further, the AAFC's appeal was compromised by the dominance of the Browns, which compiled a regular-season record of 47–4–3 and won all four league championship games. The NFL, on the other hand, was spiced with close division races from 1946 to 1949. During those years, the Cardinals and the Eagles won their first NFL championships.

In addition to adopting three AAFC teams, the NFL in 1950 adopted that league's rule allowing unlimited substitutions on any play. In 1946, the NFL had restricted substitutions to no more than three players at a time, partly because purists objected to "platoon" football. This change paved the way for the sixty-minute men, such as Eagles center and middle linebacker Chuck Bednarik, who played both offense and defense. When free substitutions were restored, they facilitated the NFL's specialization that has vastly improved the quality of play.

Bell also helped the NFL find its way in the television age. Executives in pro sports at first approached the new medium gingerly, uncertain if extra revenues from rights fees would exceed receipts lost at the gate. When Bell saw a dramatic dip in home attendance when the Rams televised their home games in 1950, he ordered a league-wide blackout of home games. The U.S. Department of Justice responded with a restraint of trade complaint, but in a U.S. District Court in Philadelphia, Judge Allan K. Grim upheld Bell's television policy in 1953. That policy would stay in place until 1973, when Congress required that any NFL game sold out seventy-two hours before kickoff be televised locally. "Way before Pete, he recognized that TV was going to be the future," Upton Bell said. "He understood the past, he dealt with the present but he was well into the future. I don't think anybody else had that kind of mind."

Though Bell strongly favored league-wide sharing of television revenues, NFL owners did not come around to that opinion until Rozelle took office. They were content to cut their own deals, and in 1956 each of the twelve teams had its own contract. Several attracted strong regional audiences. Once the Browns joined the NFL in 1950, they played in six straight championship games and won three of them. Other marquee teams included the Rams, Bears, Giants, and Colts. The Giants' rise as a perennial contender proved timely for the NFL. They played in the league's largest TV market, and their 47–7 rout of the Bears in the 1956 championship game gave the league tremendous exposure. Though disparities in TV money existed between the large and small markets, several teams were earning significant broadcast income while blackouts of home games helped the league set attendance records each year.

Bell's TV policy also prohibited cameras from showing fights, which struck critics as stodgy and even hypocritical, considering the league's rough play of the late 1950s. Bell told *Sports Illustrated*,

I don't believe for the best interests of football or the best interests of women and children who watch football it should

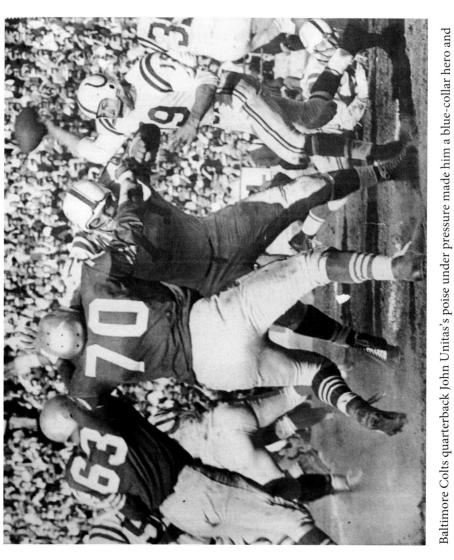

Baltimore Colts quarterback John Unitas's poise under pressure made him a blue-collar hero and a Hall of Fame quarterback. *Transcendental Graphics*

Charlie Conerly arrived in New York in 1948, before players wore facemasks, and spent fourteen seasons at quarterback for the Giants, the NFL's flagship franchise. *Transcendental Graphics*

Don Meredith, an All-America quarterback at SMU, was drafted and
hotly pursued by the NFL and AFL teams in Dallas in 1959. He finally
signed with the Cowboys. *Transcendental Graphics*

This leaping catch highlighted the versatility of New York Giants halfback Frank Gifford. Talented and handsome, he brought the NFL recognition and glamour. *Transcendental Graphics*

Pete Rozelle was a surprising choice as NFL commissioner, yet proceeded to bring the league unprecedented profits and popularity. *Transcendental Graphics*

Vince Lombardi turned the Green Bay Packers into a dynasty, thanks to such stars as halfback Paul Hornung (left), quarterback Bart Starr (middle), and fullback Jim Taylor (right). *Transcendental Graphics*

Chicago Bears Coach and Owner George Halas exerted a powerful influence on the NFL. He tried to crush the fledgling AFL by urging expansion to Dallas and Minneapolis. *Transcendental Graphics*

Coach Tom Landry, flanked here by general manager Tex Schramm (left) and co-owner Bedford Wynne, turned the Dallas Cowboys into "America's Team." *Transcendental Graphics*

Weeb Ewbank gives a chalk talk to a few Baltimore Colts players. He guided them to the 1958 NFL championship by winning "The Greatest Game Ever Played." *Transcendental Graphics*

The first seven AFL owners met in 1959. In front, left to right, are Bob Howsam (Denver), Max Winter (Minneapolis), Lamar Hunt (Dallas) and Bud Adams (Houston). Behind them, from the left, are Barron

be shown. We're selling a product just like, say, Atlantic Refining is selling one. You don't see them putting out a story about a bad situation or a bad month, do you? The people who want to watch fights, let them tune in on Wednesday night [to boxing matches].

But when the AFL began showing fights on its telecasts, the NFL followed suit.

When it came to troubleshooting, Bell was at his best. The league moved the failed New York Yanks to Dallas in 1952, but as the Texans the team fared no better. They won one game, went broke, and gave the franchise back to the league. The team was moved to Baltimore, where fans were enthusiastically buying season tickets, despite the lack of an owner. Bell turned his charm on Carroll Rosenbloom, his summer neighbor at the New Jersey shore and a player at Penn when Bell was an assistant coach there. Rosenbloom was reluctant to buy the team, but he finally capitulated when Bell promised to arrange favorable financing for Rosenbloom and his partners. He also recruited Don Kellett as the club's general manager. The Colts would give Bell the greatest day of his regime.

Bell needed to fix the Rams, too. Their ownership was so badly split between two factions that they agreed in 1956 that each side would have an equal vote on any issue and Bell would have to break any ties. The feuding drove away General Manager Tex Schramm in 1957, and the two camps could not agree on a replacement. Bell recommended Rozelle, a former Rams publicity director who was working for a public relations firm. Bell could not have known that he was also bringing the next commissioner back to the league. While Rozelle was the NFL's most accomplished commissioner, Bell by far has been the most colorful.

Upton Bell described his father:

As a commissioner, he was larger than life. There's no way you can capture a guy who was born to wealth, yet was willing to give up his standing in life and hang out on the corners. He was a guy who walked with kings and giants but he was just as happy on the street because he learned from people.

Frances Upton Bell remembered her husband in a similar vein.

He was an incredible man. He was plain and we never could get him to dress up and be a fashion plate. He liked to be with the workingman, be they plumbers or service station operators or the men who used to congregate at Davis's store. He had some pals he would have coffee with on the way to the office. They called themselves the Narberth Sunrise Society. I believe some of those men knew as much about the affairs of the league as he did because he discussed it with them.

Football, she recalled, never was far from her husband's mind. "We were on our honeymoon, or maybe it was shortly after, walking the boardwalk at Atlantic City," she said. "The night was beautiful. I said to Bert, 'Gee, look at the moon.' He looked up and said, 'Frances, I only wish I had a punter who could kick that high.'"

Halas once asked Bell and Rooney, both close friends, to check out his daughter Virginia's fiancé. In her senior year at Drexel University in Philadelphia, she began dating Ed McCaskey, a senior at Penn. Halas, who wasn't called "Papa Bear" for nothing, was especially dubious of the match because McCaskey sang in nightclubs. Rooney and Bell visited a Philadelphia nightspot in 1942 to hear McCaskey sing and size him up. Halas told Rooney that he didn't like singers, and Rooney replied he felt the same way. Bell and Rooney liked McCaskey, however. "My father called back and said he was all right," Steelers board chairman Dan Rooney recalled. "But I'm not sure that's what George wanted to hear." The couple finally eloped and was married February 2, 1943.

Though Rozelle is credited for building the NFL's crack public relations operation, Bell was no slouch in that area. He made annual visits to each training camp, and in addition to warning players about gamblers and seedy establishments, Bell told them to be courteous with sportswriters. "I don't want to hear any of you guys charging for interviews or getting in arguments with Joe King or Ed Prell or Hughie Brown or Harold Weissman," Bell would say. "Those guys and the rest of the writers give you a million dollars' worth of free publicity."

Giants Hall of Fame linebacker Sam Huff said he always appreciated Bell's visit to training camp. "So you knew there really was a Bert Bell," Huff said. "He'd say, 'Guys, I represent you and I represent the owners. If you have any problems, call me collect.' Did Pete Rozelle do that? No. That's one of the best things the commissioner ever did." Huff did have one bone to pick with Bell, however, after taking him up on his offer to call collect. "Then he wouldn't accept the call," Huff said, laughing. "You'd be told, 'Mr. Bell's not in.'"

Bell once walked into the media room at an annual league meeting in Philadelphia and asked reporters what they wanted for lunch. "Who wants sandwiches?" he asked. "Who wants chocolate ice cream? Who wants beer? Order what you want, boys. It's on the Eagles. They made all the money this year."

It's doubtful there will be another NFL commissioner as chummy as Bell was with the players. He fined Frank (Bucko) Kilroy, a roughneck middle guard for the Eagles, for kicking Bears guard Ray Bray in the groin during a 1948 exhibition game. One day, Bell met Kilroy's wife, Dorothy, on a Philadelphia street and told her: "I'm going to give that money back to your husband, but the only way he gets it is if he buys you a fur coat. Go pick one out. Then I'll give him the money with the stipulation he pays the bill."

Bell's executive style was often considered quaint. He stayed close to home, kept the league's business in his head, and preferred phone calls to written correspondence. When Rozelle became commissioner and was asked how his operation might differ from Bell's, he joked, "I think I'll have files." According to Upton Bell, though, his father was just trying to protect the league's privacy.

He said, "I do everything by phone, that way you're not leaving tracks." He kept copious notes on yellow pads and I can guarantee you he was the only one who could read them. People talk about how he'd run the league out of his house. He worked in the office, then came home and worked all night long.

Bell's workaholic schedule and failure to take better care of himself took a toll. He collapsed in 1954, prompting the Redskins' Marshall to say, "We're as much concerned about his health as Republicans are about the health of the President." Bell suffered a mild heart attack in February 1959 and was advised to reduce his workload and change his diet. His fatal collapse came eight months later, and the league's treasurer Austin Gunsel replaced him until a permanent replacement would be elected in January 1960.

Bell did not plan on staying in office past 1959. Just three days after his death, he was scheduled to sign papers for financing that would enable him to buy the Eagles again and leave the team to his sons, Upton and Bert Jr. That deal would have been timely because the Eagles were on the upswing and would win the NFL championship in 1960. "He wasn't feeling well and wanted to know his kids had something," Upton Bell recalled. "He made the deal to buy the Eagles, unbeknownst to us. He had made the decision he was going to quit and revive the team he founded."

Bell was inducted into the Pro Football Hall of Fame as part of its charter class in 1963. Perhaps no other commissioner could have moved professional football so far or so fast as Bell had in almost fourteen years. But for the NFL to take the next step, it would need a commissioner to move the league office to New York, expand his staff, and revolutionize the league's approach toward television. It would need, in other words, another commissioner who would give his life to the job. Rozelle did just that, and he died from brain cancer at age seventy, just seven years after announcing his retirement on March 22, 1989. He passed the torch to Taliabue on November 5.

"Everything that happened to my father eventually happened to Pete," said Upton Bell, who interviewed Rozelle for a Boston television station shortly before he left office.

> He said, "I don't want to wind up like your father. I want to get out when I can." It was a great feeling for me to go in and talk to my father's successor and hear the same things you kind of knew about Bert Bell. But Pete was sick a lot of the time. The job kills you sooner or later. People look at sports and think it's all fun and games. It's serious business—so many people you have to deal with and so many people you have to please. I think it killed Pete. He died much too young. But so did Bert Bell.

6

Camelot

The day that Bert Bell died, his eventual successor, Pete Rozelle, was in Chicago, watching the Los Angeles Rams defeat the Bears 28–21. It was the Rams' first win of the 1959 season, and for Rozelle, their general manager, it had to come as a huge relief. He had taken dead aim at a championship by making one of the biggest trades in NFL history, only to see the Rams lose their first two games. Any relief that Rozelle might have felt was short lived, however; he was about to experience one of the rare failures of his storied NFL career.

During his three years as the Rams' general manager, Rozelle could not approach the overwhelming success he would achieve during his nearly three decades as NFL commissioner. After squaring their record at 2–2, the 1959 Rams lost their last eight games, ending the Rozelle years with records of 6–6, 8–4, and 2–10. "Rozelle managed to destroy a great football team and lead it into the cellar in just three years," Tex Schramm said in his biography by Bob St. John. "But I guess that's what qualifies him to be commissioner."

Schramm at various times served as Rozelle's mentor, confidant, antagonist, and Hall of Fame presenter. He also preceded Rozelle as the Rams' general manager and left him with a losing team. The Rams finished 4–8 in 1956, Schramm's last season, and tied for last place in the

Western Conference. The Rams at first progressed under Rozelle and finished just one game behind the first-place Baltimore Colts in 1958.

Rozelle aimed to push the Rams to the next level by sending seven players and two 1960 draft choices to the Chicago Cardinals for fullback Ollie Matson on March 23, 1959. Rozelle's ties to Matson went back to the University of San Francisco, where Matson was a star and Rozelle the sports publicist. The trade received positive initial reviews because Matson's addition to Coach Sid Gillman's already potent offense promised to put the Rams in the championship hunt. "It's axiomatic in trading that it is necessary to give up talent to get talent and on paper this appears to be a trade that will materially help both teams," Rozelle said.

In his debut season as a Ram, Matson rushed for 863 yards, third most in the league, and six touchdowns. But the Rams were riddled by injuries and Matson could not save their season or Gillman's job. "I thought at the outset of the season we would win the championship," Rams partner Ed Pauley said. "We spend more money to win titles than any other team in the league."

The deal for Matson kept looking worse as he rushed for just 351 yards in his last three seasons in Los Angeles, but Rozelle had not exactly given away the farm. The Cardinals' haul, as detailed in Dan Daly and Bob O'Donnell's *The Pro Football Chronicle*, included four linemen: offensive tackle Ken Panfil, defensive end Glenn Holtzman, and defensive tackles Frank Fuller and Art Hauser. All except Hauser were starters.

The Rams also gave up three players from their 1959 draft: running backs Don Brown and Larry Hickman in the second and third rounds, respectively, and defensive end John Tracey in the fourth round. Finally, Rozelle traded 1960 picks that the Cardinals used for guard Mike McGee in the second round and end Silas Woods in the fourth. Yet, from this vast stockpile, Panfil proved the Rams' only notable loss. When Matson finished his career in 1966 with the Philadelphia Eagles, the only other active player involved in the famous deal was Tracey, who by then was a Buffalo Bills linebacker.

The Pro Football Chronicle pointed out that Rozelle actually made a worse deal in 1959 by trading linebacker Larry Morris, the Rams' first-round pick in 1955, for Gene Brito, the Washington Redskins' thirty-three-year-old defensive end. Brito suffered a broken leg in the second game of the 1959 season and played just one more year. Morris became a defensive stalwart for the Bears and made a key interception return in their 14–10 victory over the New York Giants in the 1963 NFL championship game.

Rozelle also took heat for trading quarterback Norm Van Brocklin, who would lead the Eagles to the NFL championship in 1960. Van Brocklin was miffed that Gillman refused to let him call his own plays, as many quarterbacks of that era did. Gillman, in turn, was less than enamored with Van Brocklin after he threw six interceptions in the 1955 NFL title-game loss and the coach made Bill Wade the primary starter in 1956. Van Brocklin remained angry with Gillman, even after he regained the starting job in 1957, and announced he was retiring in May 1958.

Rozelle traded him later that month for two players and the Eagles' first-round pick in 1959. The Rams won with Wade in 1958 and then collapsed in 1959. Rozelle was well stocked with draft choices even after the Matson trade, but he failed to lay the foundation for a winner. The Rams had six straight losing seasons after Rozelle became commissioner in January 1960 and did not turn the corner until George Allen arrived in 1966.

Even as the Rams hit bottom, most observers did not share Schramm's harsh appraisal of Rozelle's performance. As they fell to 2–7 in 1959, Jeanne Hoffman wrote in the *Los Angeles Times*: "If the Los Angeles Rams could get things done with half the precision of their general manager, Pete Rozelle, they might not be hovering around the NFL cellar these days."

On his best days and even worst days, Rozelle's legendary ability to deal with disparate personalities usually came to the fore. When he wanted Gillman to stop ignoring his assistants' advice on game day, he told his coach: "We're paying for a telephone you're not using. It costs us fifteen dollars every Sunday to run a direct line from your bench to your assistants in the press box. How can I justify this expense to the owners when you never pick up the phone?" Gillman agreed to start answering the phone. If persuasion failed, Rozelle could get tough. When he saw Rams guard and team captain Duane Putnam hanging around at midnight on the eve of a road game, Rozelle told him to go to bed. When Putnam refused, the general manager sent him home.

Rozelle's best work for the Rams, and later for the league, was achieved on the business side. The Rams drew an NFL all-time record home crowd of 102,368 fans when the San Francisco 49ers visited in 1957. The Rams' home crowds also topped 100,000 twice in 1958. When it came to marketing, Rozelle was aggressive and imaginative. He formed a partnership with Larry Kent and Roy Rogers, Inc., to license Rams souvenirs. As was typical of Rozelle, this transaction had vast and lucrative ramifications for pro football.

When the Rams suggested to Bell that this licensing deal be applied to the entire NFL, he appointed Rozelle, Bears owner George Halas, and Baltimore Colts owner Carroll Rosenbloom to consider a league-wide plan. The result was National Football League Enterprises, formed October 1, 1959, to market official league merchandise. When Rozelle became commissioner, he convinced owners to turn over their merchandising to NFL Properties, Inc. He also urged owners to bankroll NFL Films in 1965. Founded by Ed Sabol and taken over by his son, Steve, NFL Films opened the window to pro football's sights and sounds. Both companies have helped fuel the league's growth.

"[Rozelle] was always over-qualified for whatever job he took," said Bob Oates, a longtime pro football writer at the Los Angeles Times. "He was a better general manager than he was a publicist, and he was a better commissioner than he was a general manager."

Despite Rozelle's commanding legacy, the city in which he grew up and cut his teeth in pro football has become the skeleton in the NFL's closet. How could the nation's number one sports league lose its presence in the nation's second-largest market? That has been a riddle for the NFL since the end of the 1994 season, when the Raiders left Los Angeles to return to Oakland and the Rams bolted Anaheim for a sweetheart deal in St. Louis.

Beyond the ten million people in its greater metropolitan area and vast television market, Los Angeles drips with NFL history. The Rams changed the face of pro football as much as any franchise in the past sixty years. They revolutionized pro football's passing game. Rozelle became the most influential commissioner in any professional sport. Schramm used the experience he gained as the Rams' general manager to organize the Dallas Cowboys and make them one of the NFL's most successful franchises of all time. Before the 1946 season, their debut in Los Angeles, the Rams signed the first two African American players in the NFL's modern era.

Van Brocklin's 554 yards passing in the Rams' 1951 opener against the New York Yanks set a single-game record that still stood nearly six decades later. According to Bears coach and owner George Halas, the NFL came out of its dead-ball era on December 2, 1951, when the Rams routed the Bears 42–17 in Chicago. Bob Waterfield, who alternated with Van Brocklin, dropped back in his end zone and completed a ninety-one-yard touchdown pass to Elroy (Crazy Legs) Hirsch. Without even breaking stride, Hirsch made the catch in front of the Bears' bench.

"That play demonstrated the big change that had come about in T-formation football," Halas wrote in his biography. "Almost without realizing it, we had reached the point where the pass-catching end had replaced the running back as the long-distance threat. There wasn't a back in the league who could have run ninety-one yards against us."

The Rams were flashy off the field, too. They brought Hollywood to the NFL. Hirsch played himself in a 1953 movie, *Crazy Legs, All American*, and appeared in two other films. He had his own local daily radio show and weekly television show. Waterfield was the husband of sex symbol Jane Russell, one of three Hollywood actresses married to

Rams players. Comedian Bob Hope was a minority owner. With their championship teams, fabled heroes, and faded glory, the old Rams stand as the NFL's "Camelot."

They rewrote the NFL record book in 1950 by scoring 38.8 points per game. They used a spread formation that gave Van Brocklin and Waterfield three game-changing targets. Tom Fears caught eighty-four passes, including an NFL single-game record of eighteen against the Green Bay Packers. In that season, Hirsch and Glenn Davis each caught forty-two passes.

The 1950 Rams, coached by Joe Stydahar, lost the NFL champion-ship game, 30–28, to the Cleveland Browns. They won the title a year later after beating the Browns 24–17. But the coach was soon gone in one of the many soap-opera episodes that typified the Rams throughout the decade. Stydahar became convinced that assistant coach Hampton Pool was trying to undermine him and one game into the 1952 season told owner Dan Reeves that one of them had to go. When Reeves refused to fire Pool, Stydahar resigned. Pool, who had assembled the Rams' high-flying offense, took over and lasted only three seasons. Schramm, promoted from publicity director to general manager in 1954, was assigned to find Pool's replacement. He hired a little-known coach who would earn a place in the Pro Football Hall of Fame.

Schramm approached marquee name coaches, including the University of Oklahoma's Bud Wilkinson. He recommended Gillman, a big winner at the University of Cincinnati after serving as Earl Blaik's offensive line coach at West Point. According to author David Maraniss, while Gillman was cleaning out his office at Army, he was introduced to a Fordham assistant coach who was applying for the vacant job. He was Vince Lombardi, one of Fordham's "Seven Blocks of Granite" in the 1930s. When Lombardi went to shake Blaik's hand, the coach said, "Sid, take a look at the hands on this man. Easy to see why he was a block of granite."

Though Schramm had never heard of Gillman, he came highly recommended. In St. John's *Tex!* Schramm said,

Blaik told me Gillman was an excellent choice. [UCLA coach] Red Sanders told me the same thing. Everywhere I'd turn, the name "Gillman" would come up. Some people told me the only reason he hadn't landed a head job at a larger school was because he was Jewish. Those things happened in those days, but I'd never thought about that. It never was a factor.

Gillman coached the Rams to first place in the Western Conference in 1955, though they lost 38-14 to the Browns in the NFL championship game. He quickly displayed the offensive imagination that would lead to his legacy as the father of pro football's modern passing game. Gillman used small packages of specialists on both offense and defense, which he had done at Cincinnati. He started the "belly" series, in which the quarterback placed the ball in a back's stomach and sometimes pulled it back and rolled out to hand it off to a trailing back. He introduced zone blocking, which requires a lineman to block an area rather than a specific defender. Gillman had only one more winning season with the Rams, however, and was fired after the disastrous 1959 season. He never could have guessed that his most glorious coaching days were soon to follow and that he would leave an impact on the game that would be felt for decades.

Dick Vermeil, whose Eagles staff included Gillman when they reached the Super Bowl in the 1980 season, said,

Sid was a guy who felt, deep down, that people spent too much time trying to make four yards. Sid would say, "I've never seen anybody work harder to make four yards than you do, Vermeil." We put a lot of time and detail into everything we did. Sid encouraged me and taught me how to think differently. It gradually grew to where I see games and wonder, "Why the hell are they trying to make two yards for?"

The American Football League was under construction in 1959, and Barron Hilton, a hotel magnate who owned the Los Angeles Chargers, asked Oates, then with the *Los Angeles Examiner*, if he might recommend a head coach. The Rams had just fired Gillman. "I told him," Oates recalled, "'Sid Gillman is as good a coach as you could have, at least to start out with.' And he went along with that."

Oates might have rescued a brilliant coaching career. Gillman considered becoming a stockbroker in New York until the Chargers' general manager Frank Leahy asked him to meet with Hilton and discuss the head coaching job. "I had an understanding with Sid Gillman," Hilton said. "He wasn't going to tell me how to run the hotel business, and I wasn't going to tell him how to run the football club. And that arrangement worked out just fine. He was really a professor when it came to football."

Gillman's classroom immediately started rocking, and he led the Chargers to the AFL's inaugural championship game. Crowds were sparse in Los Angeles, however, and his team moved to San Diego in 1961. Gillman proceeded to make a name for himself, the Chargers, and the entire AFL with pass-happy, high-scoring games. Gillman said,

> The big play comes from the pass. God bless those runners because they get you the first down, give you ball control and keep your defense off the field. But if you want to ring the cash register, you have to pass. We're not going to throw long promiscuously, but we want people to fear our long game. Some feel if you throw short, you open up the long pass. I approach it exactly the opposite. Once we throw long successfully, then we can throw short. We'll have our five receivers going into five different areas. They'll run their patterns with enthusiasm because no receiver is a decoy. Each knows that as the pattern develops, he could be the one who gets the ball.

Gillman used his running game and short passes to stretch defenses horizontally and a deep passing game to stretch them vertically.

He coached his quarterbacks to take precise drops and hit receivers on their breaks. Because defenses became weary chasing the Chargers' receivers, they would be softened up when the Chargers started to run. "It's such a timing-oriented system," respected offensive coordinator Mike Martz told chi.scoutt.com.

> You want to get the ball downfield, yes. But you want to get it out quickly, and the timing portion is critical. There are no shades of gray. You've got to run in and out of your break—boom, like that—and you've got to be exactly where you're supposed to be. I was a San Diego high school kid in those days. I used to love to sit in old Balboa Stadium and watch his offense at work. It was an awesome experience.

Gillman's signature achievement was a 51-10 victory over the Boston Patriots for the 1963 AFL championship. His game plan, which he called "Feast or Famine," produced 610 yards against a defense that in the regular season held the Chargers to twenty-four points in two hard-fought San Diego victories. "In order to counteract their blitzes, we were determined to use a great deal of motion," Gillman explained. "We hoped to disturb their system of coverage by forcing a linebacker out of position and thus stopping their blitz. We also thought a man in motion would make Boston more vulnerable on trap plays." Gillman sent star halfback Paul Lowe in motion, clearing the way for fullback Keith Lincoln to rush for 206 yards.

Gillman's original Chargers coaching staff included two other future Hall of Famers—Chuck Noll and Al Davis. Both also won by throwing deep. Though Noll's four Super Bowl champions in Pittsburgh during the 1970s were built initially with dominating defenses and a powerful running game, his quarterback Terry Bradshaw was one of the best deep passers of all time. Davis, who has been the Raiders' coach, general manager, and owner, always has been fond of throwing deep. "Sid Gillman brought class to the AFL," Davis said. "Being part of Sid's organization was like going to a laboratory for the highly developed science of professional football."

Gillman's laboratory was visited by Don Coryell, head coach at San Diego State from 1961 through 1972, and Coryell's offensive assistants Joe Gibbs and Ernie Zampese. Gillman's offense influenced "Air Coryell," the dazzling attack that Coryell brought to the St. Louis Cardinals and then the Chargers from 1978 through 1986. Gibbs added his own wrinkles to the Gillman and Coryell offenses in the 1980s and coached the Washington Redskins to three Super Bowl wins in ten years. Zampese used the old San Diego offense to help the Dallas Cowboys win a Super Bowl when he served as Barry Switzer's offensive coordinator in 1995. No wonder Vermeil, a former Rams assistant and UCLA head coach, considered Gillman's advice so valuable.

"I had met him but I didn't know him," recalled Vermeil, who asked Gillman to join the Eagles in 1979.

> I was running the offense myself, was in charge of personnel and all that other stuff, and I needed some help. I'd been exposed to [Rams coaches] Chuck Knox and George Allen and Tommy Prothro and felt I needed another exposure, more like a Sid Gillman approach. When I approached him, he was almost seventy years old. Almost everybody I talked to said I shouldn't hire him. They thought he was stubborn and overbearing. Al Davis and [Redskins coach] Jack Pardee were the only ones who said, "Hire him." And I figured there'd be nobody more stubborn than me.

Vermeil, complaining of burnout, left the Eagles after the 1982 season. He sat out fourteen seasons before taking over the St. Louis Rams in 1997. For two years, his defense was dismal and his offense struggled, and he seemed on the verge of getting fired. Then the Rams received an offensive taste of old San Diego. Martz was hired in 1999 and installed an offense dubbed "The Greatest Show on Turf." Buoyed also by a maturing defense, the Rams earned a 23-16 Super Bowl victory over the Tennessee Titans. "The foundation of the offense we ran in 1999 was really Don Coryell," Vermeil said. "But Sid Gillman had a strong influence on all that stuff."

Schramm actually made his first Hall of Fame hire long before he found Gillman. When the Rams moved to Los Angeles in 1946, they set up training camp at Compton Junior College. Rozelle was a student who also served as Compton's sports publicist for $50 a month and assisted the Rams. His training camp jobs included pasting photos of Rams players on cardboard for a montage in an intra-squad game program. Rozelle completed his degree at the University of San Francisco while working part-time as the school's sports information director.

After graduation, he became a full-time sports publicist and assistant athletic director to Joe Kuharich for $200 a month. Rozelle found plenty of grist for his publicity mill as the Dons' football team finished 9-0 in 1951, but financial problems forced San Francisco to drop its football program in 1952. That year, the Rams needed a publicity director to replace Tex Maule, who joined the first-year Dallas Texans. Schramm called Rozelle, whom he knew from phone conversations about the Dons' professional prospects.

"I was greatly impressed with his hustle, his thoroughness," Schramm recalled. "Certain people just make a good impression on you, and Pete was one of those." Rozelle grew up in South Gate, a Los Angeles suburb, and was excited about the chance to work for the Rams—until Schramm made a disappointing salary offer. "I'm prepared to pay you $5,500," he said.

"I'm making almost that much now," Rozelle replied. "Could you make it an even $6,000?"

"No," replied Schramm. "Money isn't everything."

Rozelle accepted the job. He got along fine with Schramm, except for the time he was asked to justify an expense account. "Tex, you had this job," Rozelle said. "Don't you remember how much those [newspapermen] drink? We go over to Hudlow's, and they drink the place dry, and I have to keep up with them." Rozelle's famed powers of persuasion were visible already.

Rozelle left the Rams in 1955 to join P. K. Macker and Company, an international public relations firm run by Ken Macker, the best man at Rozelle's wedding. Macker's upbeat opinion of Rozelle would be echoed in the football world over the next few decades. In David Harris's *The League: The Rise and Decline of the NFL*, Macker said,

> I've never met anybody that has more captivated me, then or since. Pete was a bright, interesting young man. I was extraordinarily impressed by him. I needed a strong partner and I talked him into joining. I don't know anybody with an unkind word to say about him. He doesn't get blinded or sidetracked. He keeps his thinking process on the road all the time. He was always self-assured, always a man who could make a decision and live with it.

Rozelle's biggest account for Macker was the 1956 Olympic Games in Melbourne. Australian organizers were getting poor reviews for their state of preparedness and needed their image polished, especially in the United States, then the power center of the Olympic movement. "Rozelle immediately took the mayor of Melbourne around the country and within two weeks, the feeling was totally reversed," Macker said. Rozelle also escorted reporters from major U.S. media outlets to Melbourne and showed them the Olympic facilities. In addition, Rozelle handled the games' international media relations. Clearly, he could have enjoyed a long and successful public relations career.

But he was drawn back to pro football in 1957 when Bell, the commissioner, recruited him to become the Rams' general manager. Schramm grew weary of feuding among the Rams' owners and quit to work for CBS Sports. Though Reeves had a brilliant football mind, he constantly created turmoil. When he moved the Rams from Cleveland, he was majority owner, with Fred Levy Jr. as his partner. However, Reeves soon became strapped for cash. He had lost $50,000 in 1945, his last year in Cleveland, though the Rams had defeated the Washington Redskins 15-14 in the NFL championship game. When he moved West, Reeves's losses mounted, partly because he was competing with the Los Angeles Dons. An original member of the All-America Football Conference, the Dons began playing in 1946.

In 1947, Reeves took in three new partners: Ed Pauley, Harold Pauley, and Hal Seley. Each received a share of the Rams for a dollar and agreed to share future losses. The new partners constantly bickered with Reeves, who drank heavily, and they eventually won over Levy as an ally. This split created a stalemate over important club matters. Schramm walked an uneasy line between both factions when he served as the general manager for three years, and they were as divided as ever when picking his replacement. The dissension was so bitter that both sides had to agree that Bell would break any deadlocks. The commissioner, who knew Macker and remembered Rozelle as a crack publicist for the Rams, proposed that the team hire Rozelle. "You're the first thing they've agreed on since [President James] Garfield was shot," Bell told the new general manager.

Rozelle's dedication to his new post was evident when the Rams opened the 1958 season at home against the Browns on September 28. His daughter, Anne Marie, was born during halftime, and Rozelle rushed back to the Los Angeles Memorial Coliseum for the second half. "We were ahead when she was born," he said, "but I wasn't able to pass out cigars for a double victory. By the time I got to the game, we had wound up with a 30-27 loss. We lost a football game, but I gained a daughter."

Rozelle's first wife, Jane, once tried to get his mind off football by taking him to an art museum near the coliseum. "I bought a modernistic print of a shoe," she said. "Pete took one look at the print and said, 'Now, why did you buy that? It'll make me think of Lou Groza.'" A sixteen-yard field goal by Groza in the final minute cost the Rams the NFL championship in 1950, just one of the many storied and stormy years of the Reeves era.

Both Rozelle and Schramm, two of the most influential executives in the modern NFL, owed much of their success to Reeves. After his first season in Los Angeles, Reeves fired general manager Chile Walsh and ran the team himself. He hired Schramm as his publicity director on the recommendation of *Los Angeles Times* sports editor Paul Zimmerman, who had hired Schramm for one summer. Schramm faced an uphill climb because the Rams attracted fewer fans during their first three years than did the Dons, who did not even play in the coliseum.

"Everybody was talking about what a gutsy move it was for Reeves," said Schramm, a native Californian who was finishing up his degree at the University of Texas in 1946.

> Hell, the move seemed logical to me. I didn't see the big deal. I thought the sun rose and set in Southern California. We had better college football than anybody else, year in and year out. We had the Olympics, the Rose Bowl, and the top track and field meets. To me, the rest of the country was backward, so why not move to Los Angeles? But I was still young. Later, I realized that it did take a lot of guts. Others were aware of the potential on the West Coast but were just afraid to be the first to try it. They wanted to see what happened to somebody else first. But the fans were there, the money was there.

Schramm's knack for promotion became evident when Rams halfback Fred Gehrke, an industrial design artist in the off-season, suggested in 1948 that a ram's horn become the team emblem. Schramm asked Gehrke to come up with a design, and he painted a leather helmet blue with a gold ram's horn on each side. Reeves approved the new look, and the Rams became the first professional team ever to have an emblem on its helmets. Gehrke stuck with football, however, and became the Denver Broncos' general manager in 1977.

Reeves was a pioneer in scouting and involved his entire front office in draft preparation. This education would help Schramm move the Dallas Cowboys to the cutting edge of talent evaluation in the 1970s. Though the draft had been around since 1935, there were no full-time NFL scouts until Reeves hired Ed Kotal. He scouted year around, and by 1955, the Rams had a network of some 100 college coaches who filed scouting reports.

"Reeves taught Schramm, who taught Rozelle," Oates recalled. "Reeves was clearly ahead of everybody in the league in almost every phase of the game, except he didn't have much patience. That was his undoing."

Reeves's thoroughness helped him steal Van Brocklin in the fourth round of the 1949 draft. Van Brocklin was a standout at Oregon who was generally expected to complete his college career in 1949; however, the Rams knew he was eligible to be drafted because he had completed his degree in summer school. Van Brocklin had married his biology lab instructor and needed to start earning a living. The Rams drafted him with the thirty-seventh overall pick.

The Rams also were the first team to systematically mine small-college talent. Schramm started the Tom Harmon Little All-American team, ostensibly an effort to give small-school stars their due. It was, in fact, a scheme to compile scouting data on obscure players. A legendary player at the University of Michigan and a Rams player when they first moved to Los Angeles, Harmon lent his name to the team and signed the plaques. Small-college coaches around the nation nominated the players.

Schramm explained,

We felt the best way to do this was to have all the coaches list the top five players they'd played against. This would give us more objectivity than if they chose their own players. We also had them fill in the height, weight and time in the hundred-yard dash. Nobody had paid any attention to the small colleges before, so we got a helluva response.

This information unearthed some terrific talent. From Arnold College in Connecticut, the Rams picked Andy Robustelli, a future Hall of Fame defensive end, in the nineteenth round of the 1951 draft. In 1949, they landed Grambling College running back Paul (Tank) Younger, the NFL's first African American free agent signed out of college. A year later, the Rams made Washington & Jefferson's Dan (Deacon) Towler the first African American player drafted by an NFL team. A twenty-fifth round pick, Towler led the Rams in rushing for three straight years.

The Rams made the historic signings of Washington, a halfback, and Strode, an end, in 1946. Both had been UCLA football teammates of Jackie Robinson's in 1939. By 1946, however, both Washington and Strode were past their primes. They had been shut out of the NFL by an unwritten rule against signing African Americans, and they spent their best professional seasons in the Pacific Coast League. Washington spent three years with the Rams and Strode stayed one year before finishing his career in Canada. Also in 1946, the Browns of the AAFC signed fullback Marion Motley and linebacker Bill Willis, young African American stars on the verge of Hall of Fame careers. These four signings came a year before Major League Baseball broke the color barrier. In 1946, Robinson was playing for the Brooklyn Dodgers' top minor-league affiliate in Montreal.

Washington's and Strode's signings resulted from public pressure. When Walsh, the Rams' first general manager, asked at a Coliseum Commission hearing for permission to use the stadium, African American journalist Halley Harding spoke eloquently about the NFL's exclusion of African Americans. He struck a special chord by emphasizing the league's discrimination against Washington, a hometown hero. Walsh, worried about being denied use of the coliseum, promised to give Washington a tryout. The Rams signed Washington and later added Strode. But if those deals were made out of expedience, the Rams' subsequent breakthrough signings of African American players were not.

The Rams also blazed trails by posting a draft board and rating the top fifty prospects, regardless of position. Such draft day organization is common throughout the NFL today. Recalling an era in which coaches, scouts, and general managers from all teams gathered in one city, Schramm said,

> We'd go into the draft with our books and lists, and the other teams would laugh. But, whereas the other clubs were hoping to get maybe two of the top players out of the first twenty-five [rounds], we'd be getting nine of our top fifteen, or six or seven out of our first eighteen. It was like shooting fish in a barrel.

The Rams did not need painstaking scouting to identify their primary target in the 1960 draft, their last one under Rozelle. A 2-10 record, which tied for the league's worst, entitled them to the top overall pick. Virtually every scout and general manager in pro football agreed that the top prospect was Louisiana State University halfback Billy Cannon.

Trying to hide its cards from the upstart AFL, the NFL held an unannounced draft in late November 1959, and the Rams picked Cannon. Though the star still had another college game left to play, Rozelle covertly signed him, executing a coup that promised to revive the Rams. Who knew this signing would shake the Rams, Rozelle, and the entire league to their very foundations?

7

A Provincial Lad

In the lore of Louisiana State University, Billy Cannon is the ultimate football hero. In professional football history, he is akin to Helen
of Troy, "the face that launched a thousand ships." In 1959, Cannon
signed contracts with teams in both leagues and started a seven-year
signing war.

Cannon's legendary stature was secured Halloween night 1959
when LSU, ranked first in the national polls, met second-ranked University of Mississippi in Baton Rouge. The Rebels led 3–0 in the fourth
quarter when Jake Gibbs, the Ole Miss quarterback, dropped back to
punt. Gibbs intended to kick the ball out of bounds, but it took a high
bounce to Cannon at the eleven-yard line. Although seven would-
be tacklers got their hands on him, Gibbs was the last player between
Cannon and the end zone. Gibbs made a desperate lunge, but Cannon
easily eluded him and gave LSU a 7–3 lead. Mississippi was knocking on
the door in the final minute, but Cannon assisted on a goal-line tackle
with eighteen seconds left to clinch the victory.

Cannon was voted the 1959 Heisman Trophy winner, the first ever
from LSU, and accepted the award from Vice President Richard Nixon
in New York. He would be the first Heisman winner to field bids from
both the National Football League and the American Football League.

The Los Angeles Rams had the first pick of the NFL draft on November 30, 1959, and, to no one's surprise, they took Cannon. The Houston Oilers had selected him on November 22 as one of the territorial choices allowed by the AFL to help teams sign college stars from their areas. Players were stripped of their college eligibility, however, if they were caught signing professional contracts before their college careers ended. The NFL had assured the National Collegiate Athletic Association it would not sign players prematurely, but with two leagues chasing the same quarry, all bets were off.

AFL founder and Dallas Texans owner Lamar Hunt said in Jeff Miller's book, *Going Long*,

> In December, it came to our attention that some key players had already signed with the NFL—Billy Cannon, Johnny Robinson, Charlie Flowers—before their college eligibility was up. All three were playing in the Sugar Bowl game, so we devised a plan to get an acceptance from them and sign them on the field immediately after the game. This would not only be embarrassing to the NFL but they would not be able to defend their position. Each of the players sent notice a day or two before the game renouncing their previous commitments.

Cannon's combination of size, speed, and power would make any scout drool. He packed 225 pounds on a six-foot-one frame, ran a hundred yards in 9.4 seconds, and benched 435 pounds. "Cannon was rated number one on our draft list," said Lynn (Pappy) Waldorf, chief scout of the San Francisco 49ers. "We asked twenty-four coaches to list the ten best players in the South last year, and fifteen of them placed Cannon first. He has all the attributes to be an outstanding player in the National Football League."

This assessment is the kind of remark usually made at a draft day news conference. Waldorf, however, was testifying in U.S. district court, where it would be decided whether Cannon would play for the Rams or the Oilers. By the time Cannon's college career ended with a rematch against Mississippi in the Sugar Bowl on January 1, he had signed with both teams. It would require a judge to sort out this mess.

The skullduggery began when Rams general manager Pete Rozelle flew Cannon to Philadelphia, site of the draft. Cannon checked into the Sheraton Hotel as Billy Gunn and soon received a phone call instructing him to take a cab to the Warwick Hotel. Rozelle greeted him in the lobby and escorted him to a news conference, where Cannon was introduced as the Rams' first-round draft choice. "I've always wanted to play for the Rams since I was a little boy," he said. Rozelle then took Cannon to another room, where he signed three one-year contracts at $15,000 a year, with a $10,000 signing bonus and $500 for travel expenses. To avoid evidence that Cannon had signed before his last college game, the contract was not dated.

Back in Houston, Oilers owner Bud Adams also wanted to sign Cannon, but he could not find him, much less make him an offer. Taking what Adams described as "a wild shot," he phoned Alvin Roy, a strength and conditioning coach in Baton Rouge and Cannon's friend. Roy was evasive at first about Cannon's whereabouts. He told Adams he was busy attending football banquets.

Adams recalled saying,

> "Let me tell you something. Just tell Billy it doesn't matter if he signed with the Rams because he shouldn't have done that. He still has the Sugar Bowl to play. We'll sign him right after the game's over with. Tell him that whatever he signed for, I'll double it. Tell him to call me collect." I told my wife, "Honey, I'll bet we're going to get a call from Baton Rouge, Louisiana, in less than thirty minutes." Sure enough, about twenty-eight minutes later, he called me.

According to Adams, Cannon admitted to signing a contract with the Rams, which was approved by acting NFL commissioner Austin

Gunsel. Adams repeated his offer to double the package Cannon had received from the Rams. He offered $110,000, the first six-figure contract ever in professional football. Adams also gave Cannon a Cadillac for his father and a half interest in the Billy Cannon Oil Company, which would operate five service stations in the Baton Rouge area.

The Cadillac came into play when Cannon, reluctant to trust promises made over the phone, flew to Houston to get Adams's staggering offer in writing. Adams showed him the contract at his office and then drove Cannon to Adams's house in a white Cadillac that belonged to his wife, Nancy. Cannon said his father would be overwhelmed if he could have that car. Adams told Cannon to take the car but not to alert Nancy, who had briefly left them alone. When she came back, Adams told her that Cannon was driving home. "'How's he driving back?' she asked. I said, 'In your car,'" Adams recalled. "Then it hit the fan."

Adams assigned Adrian Burk, a former Philadelphia Eagles quarterback and a lawyer in Houston, to sign Cannon under a Tulane Stadium goalpost immediately after the Sugar Bowl. Adams would both get nationwide TV exposure for the Oilers and the AFL and make the signing appear legitimate. Adams had, in fact, already signed Cannon to a personal services contract on December 29.

Developments surrounding Cannon after the Sugar Bowl were more dramatic than the game itself, a 21–0 Ole Miss victory. Rozelle flew to New Orleans for the game and soon got wind of Cannon's deal with the Oilers, but he did not have any luck getting Cannon to meet with him. Rozelle finally caught up with Cannon in the LSU locker room, put his arm around him, and said, "Well, Billy, it's going to be awfully nice having you with us in Los Angeles." As Rozelle quickly realized, that was wishful thinking.

"I heard him tell the press he had just signed a contract with Houston," Rozelle testified in court. "I told Cannon he had a binding contract with the Rams and Cannon told me his deal with Houston is better [and] whatever happens has to happen."

The Rams sued the AFL in Los Angeles federal district court, demanding that Cannon honor his contract with them. The Rams not only lost their lawsuit but endured the embarrassment of admitting they had signed Cannon early. The case was especially embarrassing to Rozelle because by the time the case went to court, he was NFL commissioner and charged with enforcing the league's rules. When the verdict went against the Rams, it put a notch on the AFL's barrel before it even played a game.

In an amended complaint in April 1960, the Rams presented evidence of the personal services contract Cannon signed before the Sugar Bowl. This ploy was intended to prove that the Oilers' behavior was no more above board than that of the Rams. Adams countered that the personal services contract was "with me and had nothing to do with the Oilers." He claimed that Cannon's postgame agreement was the only football contract he had signed.

But a letter from Cannon to Adams, dated December 23, 1959, contradicted Adams. It read:

> I, the undersigned person do hereby bind and obligate myself to play football and perform other personal services in the management of the Billy A. Cannon Oil Company, Inc. for you. In consideration for a period of three years, I am to receive the sum of One Hundred Thousand Dollars . . . and in addition, therefore, I am to receive a sum of Ten Thousand Dollars cash and also in addition, therefore, you are to donate to my father a 1959 Cadillac automobile. A detailed contract setting out the duties and services I am to render on your behalf will be prepared and signed by me on Saturday, December 26, 1959, in Baton Rouge, Louisiana. Very truly yours, Billy A. Cannon.

Cannon had returned his bonus check to the Rams, which he accused of "fraud and deceit." He insisted that Rozelle misled him to believe the contract would not take effect until after the Sugar Bowl and until then was unenforceable. Cannon and his attorney, Lowell L. Dryden, lost their bid for a jury trial when federal judge William Lindberg ruled in mid-June that the issues were too complex for a jury to understand. "No matter what happens, Billy Cannon will never play football for the Los Angeles Rams," Dryden vowed.

The Rams, however, threatened to prevent Cannon from becoming an Oiler, at least for the length of his Rams' contract. "The Rams would be happy to have Cannon," said their attorney, John C. McHose. "But the Rams can't force him to play. However, they can enforce the negative aspects of the contract."

Dryden claimed the Rams did not want Cannon as much as they wanted to keep him from the AFL. "Cannon is the pickle in the middle of the fight between the National Football League and the American Football League," the lawyer said. "This case will be a landmark in professionals' relations with amateurs."

The suggestion that the Rams did not want Cannon was, of course, ridiculous. They debunked that claim by asking expert judges of football talent to evaluate his pro prospects. In addition to Waldorf, the Rams deposed Chicago Bears coach and owner George Halas, who said his team projected Cannon as the top prospect in the 1960 draft.

Cannon's memory did not seem as sharp as his physical tools. He said he could not remember telling Nixon during the Heisman Trophy presentation on December 10, 1959, that he was "pleased" to have been picked by the Rams. "I wouldn't say I didn't, but I don't recall," Cannon testified. Asked if he and Adams had discussed a contract to play football for the Oilers, Cannon replied, "No sir. We discussed a personal services contract."

Both sides seemed confident of a favorable verdict. "Ed Pauley was playing golf with Barron Hilton two days before the final decision in the case," Adams said, referring to the Rams' partner and Los Angeles Chargers owner. "He told Barron, 'I don't know what Adams is thinking. He can't win this case. We signed him first.'"

Judge Lindberg, however, freed Cannon from the Rams' contract because he agreed that Rozelle had taken advantage of him. "Not withstanding his prowess and ability on the gridiron, he is not an astute businessman," Lindberg ruled. "He is exceptionally naive for a college senior and a provincial lad untutored and unwise in the ways of the business world." The judge added that he found it difficult to resolve the issues in the case because Rozelle had cast a "shroud of secrecy" over negotiations. He also criticized Rozelle for allowing Cannon to bargain "without benefit of counselor advice." Lindberg also ruled the Rams' entire contract invalid because the league had approved only the first of its three years.

Rams owner Dan Reeves said he was "shocked" by the judge's harsh criticism of Rozelle. "Pete is the most honest man in the world," his former boss said. Rams general manager Elroy Hirsch, who would win some and lose some in the war between the leagues, approached Cannon after the verdict, shook his hand, and said, "Well, we wanted you, anyway." Hirsch later noted sarcastically that when Cannon testified that he did not understand the document he had signed with Rozelle, he must have missed the one-inch type that read "Standard Player's Contact." Hirsch joked, "We saved a little money. He's going to need contact lenses."

The judge's characterization of Cannon as naive provoked some folks' astonishment. "Baloney," said end Chris Burford, a Dallas Texans teammate of Johnny Robinson's, who also played with Cannon at LSU. "Billy and Johnny Robinson had a section of tickets in that stadium in Baton Rouge. They knew more [about] business than we all came across."

Tex Schramm, chief executive of a Dallas franchise hoping for admittance to the NFL in 1960, claimed he could have signed Cannon for the Cowboys. Schramm said he approached Cannon in the fall of 1959 in New York, when he was being honored as part of the Kodak All-America team. "I actually convinced him to sign with us," Schramm said. "Then I called my old friend Pete Rozelle, and told him what I had done. I figured we'd sign Cannon to a personal services contract and worry about details later."

Rozelle was outraged. "What the hell do you think you're doing?" he asked Schramm. "You start messing around like that, and I will see that you never get a franchise."

Schramm backed off but insisted, "If Rozelle had left me alone, the NFL and the Cowboys would have ended up with Billy Cannon."

A serious back injury in 1962, his third professional season, prevented Cannon from fulfilling his promise. He was named Most Valuable Player of the AFL's first championship game, a 24–16 Oilers victory over the Chargers. He led the league in rushing with 948 yards a year later, but he was never the same after his injury. He was traded to the Oakland Raiders in 1964, moved to tight end in 1967, and started in the Super Bowl that season. He was cut before the 1970 opener.

Two other players who signed with AFL teams right after the Sugar Bowl also wound up in court. Robinson, a halfback and defensive back at LSU, signed with both the Detroit Lions and the Texans while Flowers, a fullback from Mississippi, signed with the New York Giants and the Chargers. Giants co-owner Wellington Mara signed Flowers at an awards banquet in New York. Flowers was quoted as saying in Carlo DeVito's *Wellington*:

> But Mr. Mara said, "Son, if you don't want to play with the Giants, just say so, we don't want any player who doesn't want to be a Giant." I received a contract and a good bonus check from the Giants, but I sent it all back and asked Mister Mara to stand by his statement about not wanting anybody who didn't want to play with the Giants. I definitely want to play for Los Angeles. I'm plenty mad about this thing.

The court ruled that Flowers had the right to void the Giants' contract because it lacked the standard league approval. In what he called "a harmless deception," Mara concealed the contract until after the Sugar Bowl, and by then, Flowers had changed his mind. Though not as historically significant as the Cannon trial, the Flowers case was much more entertaining. It was revealed that Ed McKeever, the Giants' scout who had suggested drafting Flowers, was an AFL secret agent. He had accepted $1,000 to steer Flowers to the Chargers and also aided the defection of James Varnado, a fullback from Southern. By the time this information all came out, McKeever was general manager of the AFL's Boston Patriots. Giants coach Jim Lee Howell was called as a witness at the trial, and though known for his easygoing nature, he turned belligerent. Two U.S. marshals had to control him. "You will conduct yourself as a gentleman as long as you are in this court," the judge instructed him, according to *Going Long*. "Put your feet on the ground and restrain yourself."

Robinson was the third overall pick of the 1960 NFL draft and at first signed with the Lions. Before the Sugar Bowl, they gave him a three-year, $33,000 contract with a $2,500 signing bonus. "It was illegal to sign while still a college player but commonly done from what I understood," he said. Though Hunt offered Robinson no more than the Lions had, Robinson decided he would be more comfortable staying in the South. Robinson signed with the Texans after the Sugar Bowl, and he, too, saw his new deal upheld in court. Robinson spent his first two seasons at halfback and, after switching to safety, was named to the Pro Football Hall of Fame's All-Time All-AFL Team at that position. He made fifty-seven interceptions, leading the AFL with ten in 1966 and the NFL with ten in 1970. Flowers, meanwhile, rushed for just 338 yards in two years with the Chargers.

The court cases were only the start of the acrimony between the leagues. "You can't believe what went on," recalled Baltimore Colts owner Carroll Rosenbloom.

> Scouts would take to a hotel room kids who didn't know what
> it was to have 50 dollars, spread $5,000 in hundred dollar bills
> on the bed and say, "You sign and the money is yours." It

wasn't hard to get a signature. Then another recruiter would come along and say, "Look, we'll give you $6,000 to come with us." The kid would sign and keep the earlier $5,000. Recruiters were making bums out of nice kids.

Curtis McClinton, a running back from the University of Kansas, was among the prospects harvesting the fruits of this bidding. The Rams and Texans each made him a "future" draft choice, and Hirsch visited the Kansas campus to negotiate for the Rams. McClinton recalls that Hirsch kept implying he could get a much nicer car than the jalopy he was driving. This tactic offended McClinton, who said he felt he was being treated as a stereotypical black athlete.

McClinton, who would be AFL Rookie of the Year in 1962, said,

He was more interested in talking about cars, so I changed the subject to compensation. I told him I was interested in a multi-year, no-cut contract and I named the signing bonus. He said he never heard of a "no-cut contract." I said, "You mean to tell me you didn't read where Billy Cannon got a no-cut contract?" Right then, he and I had some distance between us. They got too pedestrian with me."

Hunt, however, struck McClinton as sincere and not patronizing. McClinton agreed to a three-year, $100,000 package. He agreed to sign after playing in the 1961 Bluebonnet Bowl in Houston. McClinton said,

The issue of the NFL and the Rams, or the AFL and the Texans, had nothing to do with my decision. It had to do with character, it had to do with money, and it had to do with Lamar. He signed me under the goalpost and gave me a check—it was ten thousand dollars. I was so excited, I didn't know what to do with it. I put it in one of my teammates' pockets.

Such fierce bidding between the leagues in the AFL's early years was just a warm-up for the outlandish, often-comical episodes of "baby-sitting," which was a euphemism for the virtual kidnapping of players to hide them from the rival league. Despite the AFL's aggressive pursuit of top players, the NFL kept waiting for the upstarts to fold. The older league perhaps sniffed victory when Hunt, despite his team's championship in 1962, moved from Dallas after that season. Hunt, however, drafted a truckload of talent in November 1962 to bring to Kansas City. He signed the first overall pick of the AFL draft, Grambling defensive tackle Buck Buchanan. He also signed the eighth overall selection, Michigan State guard Ed Budde, and seventh-round pick Bobby Bell, a linebacker from the University of Minnesota. Bell and Buchanan are Hall of Famers, and Budde was named to the All-Time All-AFL team. The Dallas Cowboys also were interested in Buchanan but could not find him to make him an offer. Hunt had stashed him in a Dallas apartment complex.

Either league would stoop to almost any stunt to snatch a blue-chip prospect. In a supposedly secret conference call two weeks before the end of the 1961 college season, AFL owners agreed how to split up the top forty-eight prospects. This agreement was soon reported in newspapers across the country, and college officials were not pleased. AFL commissioner Joe Foss, unaware the draft was being held, tried to justify it as an "intra-league negotiation rights poll." He wrote in his autobiography, *A Proud American*:

> The incident blossomed into a major scandal. Not since the beginning of the league had the NFL generated such headlines. Pete Rozelle was among the first to jump on me for allowing my owners to violate pledges to collegiate organizations, and columnists used up a forest of trees thinking of new ways to pose the question, "What sort of commissioner would be unaware of a draft by his own team owners?"

The Buffalo Bills' Ralph Wilson, one of three owners who organized the secret draft, made no apologies. "Next year is a year of decision for our league and it is of utmost importance to make a representative showing in the race for outstanding collegiate talent," he told the *New York Daily Mirror*. "I strongly supported the secret telephone poll, along with Lamar Hunt and Bud Adams, as the most practical approach to an early advantage to negotiating with players."

The secret draft, in truth, was hard to distinguish from standard operating procedure. Teams in both leagues already were targeting players before the draft and making them contract offers, if not discreetly signing them. Once an owner had a commitment from a player, no other owner in the same league would draft him. More money was thrown around each year, and neither side was ready to back off. The AFL's bargaining power enjoyed a huge boost in 1964 when it negotiated a five-year, $36 million contract with NBC that would take effect in 1965.

Norma Hunt recalls that she and Lamar were on their honeymoon at the Winter Olympics in Innsbruck, Austria, while negotiations with NBC continued in New York. Wilson was at the Olympics, too, and the group was in the Bills' owner's room when news broke that the deal was completed. "If you had seen the amount of jumping for joy in that room, you'd be amazed these serious business guys could bust loose like that," Norma Hunt recalled. "We have laughed with Ralph about that for many years." The new league was then ready to up the ante. "The AFL was much more aggressive from the standpoint of taking chances and trying to get commitments early—because we needed to be," Lamar Hunt said.

When his team was still in Dallas, Hunt pursued Roman Gabriel, a star quarterback at North Carolina State, who was taken first overall by the Oakland Raiders and second overall by the Rams in the 1962 draft. The Raiders were so strapped for cash, however, that they could not sign any draft picks and gave theirs to the Texans. When Hunt phoned Gabriel in a hotel room, however, he was being watched by Hirsch, who had offered Gabriel $15,000 a year for three years. The Rams' general manager took Hunt's call, pretended he was Gabriel, and never let on about Hunt's proposal.

"He was offering me $100,000 to come play in the AFL," Gabriel said years later. "But I didn't take the call. Elroy Hirsch did. So I ended up going to the Rams."

Hunt also was none the wiser. "I thought I was talking to Roman Gabriel," he said. "I heard years later that it was Hirsch posing as Gabriel. That was typical. All was fair in love and war and in recruiting players."

Hirsch was a forerunner for the babysitters. For the 1964 draft, which was held late in 1963, the Rams hired Bert Rose, their former publicity director and the Minnesota Vikings' first general manager, to recruit Los Angeles businessmen to get chummy with top prospects. The players would be wined, dined, and sold on the NFL while being shielded from AFL representatives. Rozelle liked the plan so much that he asked Reeves, the Rams owner, if Rose could set up this program for the entire league. It was called "Operation Baby-Sit," and for the next two seasons it provided some of the most astonishing tales in pro football history.

Scouts from NFL personnel departments performed most of the baby sitting during the 1964 season. But the next year, Rozelle turned to the corporate contacts he cultivated in New York. He recruited executives from Madison Avenue advertising agencies, who were expertly trained to deliver the NFL's pitch. Rozelle also got plenty of mileage from United Airlines, a television sponsor of NFL games. The airline supplied a Gold League pass for the baby sitters, giving them free and unlimited travel at a moment's notice. Former NFL public relations executive Don Weiss recalls seeing piles of airline tickets on a table in the NFL office shortly after he began working there in 1965. "There had to be hundreds of them, to every conceivable destination in the land," he wrote in *The Making of the Super Bowl.*

Baby sitters were assigned to contact prospects during the season and stay with them through the draft and until they signed their contracts. This work often required keeping a prospect on the move or cooped up in an out-of-the-way hotel. College players tolerated this treatment because they did not have agents to advise them and considered it a big deal to get a free trip, especially to Las Vegas or Hawaii. The baby sitters were not significantly compensated but were happy just to rub elbows with college stars and enter the glamorous world of pro football. "Each team submitted a list of about fifty players it wanted covered," recalled former Dallas Cowboys director of player personnel Gil Brandt.

AFL owners then hired their own baby sitters, which included ex-coaches, lawyers, and other professionals. The AFL's most distinguished baby sitter was Ed King, who lost tight end Milt Morin to the Cleveland Browns after the 1965 season but bounced back to become governor of Massachusetts in 1978. "It sounds incomprehensible today that we would operate that way," Hunt said. "It definitely was part of the recruiting times. It was sort of guerilla warfare—every team for itself, every man for himself, whatever it took to keep a player away from the other league. And I think it was effective."

Hunt was the winner in the most notorious baby sitting caper, the tug-of-war for Prairie View A&M wide receiver Otis Taylor. The Chiefs were pioneers in scouting historically black colleges, and a former sportswriter, Lloyd Wells, scouted those schools and helped the Chiefs become a powerhouse. Wells was Taylor's confidant, and the Chiefs expected to sign him. Taylor, a senior in 1964, met with team officials before the Chiefs played at Houston on November 22. Six days later, both leagues held their 1965 drafts.

That gap was time enough for the Cowboys to almost steal Taylor. They invited him and teammate Seth Cartwright to spend Thanksgiving weekend in Dallas for what was billed as a party for the region's top draft prospects. "It's always nice to be wanted, so I figured what the hell, and decided to go," Taylor wrote in his autobiography, *The Need to Win*. "What I didn't know—didn't even consider—was that the gathering was actually an NFL tactic to keep me and the others away from the AFL."

Unaware of this development, Wells went to Nashville to pick up two players—one of whom was Jackson State College wide receiver Gloster Richardson—and bring them to Kansas City for the draft. Wells received a call from Hunt's secretary, however, telling him that Taylor had left the Prairie View campus for Dallas. "He did the natural thing considering the combative, warlike climate that existed between the two leagues," Taylor wrote. "He panicked."

Wells flew to Dallas and began canvasing hotels, but the Cowboys moved the players daily. Further, Taylor did not go out except for one dinner date. Wells finally phoned Taylor's family in Houston and learned the name of his dinner companion. Wells reached her and learned that Taylor was at the Continental Hotel in suburban Richardson. He gave a porter $20 for the whereabouts of Taylor's room. The Cowboys kept a baby sitter in the hall, and Wells claimed he was a reporter seeking an interview with Taylor for *Ebony* magazine. When he got Taylor alone, Wells was angry. "Man, you're doing me wrong," he said. "We've been friends too long to let something like this happen." Wells added that the Chiefs had a new red Thunderbird waiting for Taylor in Kansas City once he signed a contract.

"But I didn't leave then, and I don't know why," Taylor wrote. "I was young and mixed up, and while I knew what I wanted to do, it just took me a while to finalize my decision." Taylor told Wells to come back later, but when he did, Cartwright's girlfriend answered the door and said they could not leave yet. Taylor finally called Wells in the middle of the night and left the ground-floor room through the window.

"The Cowboys always tried to be very thorough," Brandt said. "We didn't leave a guy alone except to go to the bathroom. Our guy had a few beers and went to sleep."

Taylor was flown to Kansas City, where he was drafted in the fourth round and signed with the Chiefs for a $15,000 bonus and a $15,000 salary. And the Thunderbird was indeed waiting for him. The Chiefs also signed Cartwright, but he did not make the team. Taylor became one of pro football's top receivers and was a hero of the Chiefs' 23-7 victory over the Minnesota Vikings in the January 1970 Super Bowl. "We thought Taylor was good," Brandt said. "But we had no idea how good."

No team had perfect records in these cutthroat times. The Chiefs' first-round pick that year was Gale Sayers, the standout running back from Kansas. The Chiefs offered him a contract and considered him a good bet to sign, yet draft day found the "Kansas Comet" at the Baltimore home of Buddy Young, a former NFL running back from Chicago who was working at the league office. The future Hall of Fame runner was drafted in the first round and signed by the Chicago Bears.

The Chiefs that year also had their eye on Mike Curtis, a fullback and linebacker from Duke. So did the Colts, whose baby sitter rented an entire floor of a motel near Baltimore to hide Curtis. Because Curtis's baby-sitter was monitoring his phone calls, Chiefs scout Don Klosterman had his secretary call the motel and pretend to be Curtis's fiancée. Once Curtis came on the line, she handed the phone to Klosterman, who tried to make a deal. The Colts still drafted Curtis in the first round and signed him.

Harry Schuh, an offensive tackle from Memphis State who would start for the Raiders in the second Super Bowl, was never as big a star as Sayers, Curtis, or Taylor was. But the cloak-and-dagger competition to hide him before the 1965 draft was as crazy as it would get. The Rams also wanted Schuh and assigned former head coach Hampton Pool to baby sit him. The Raiders beat Pool to the punch and flew Schuh, his wife, and infant son and several Raiders officials to Las Vegas.

Pool tried to overcome his late start by convincing Schuh's parents to report him as a kidnapping victim. The Raiders convinced Schuh's wife to call authorities and shoot down that report. Once Pool flew to Las Vegas, all the adversaries were on the scene—a scene right out of a slapstick movie. The Raiders moved the Schuhs to different hotels, yet Pool found the big tackle at a casino. The Raiders then drove him around town for four hours, but Pool found them at a hotel stage show. Finally, the Raiders flew Schuh's wife and child to Los Angeles as decoys while they took him to Hawaii. The Raiders drafted him in the first round and signed him in Hawaii. "Pool sent a telegram: 'Boo hoo. I lost my Schuh!'" Brandt recalled.

The Rams instead used their first-round pick on Washington State cornerback Clarence (Clancy) Williams. He had been babysat by three different leagues by the time the Rams finally signed him. The Chargers struck first, flying Williams to San Diego. A Rams baby sitter then brought Williams back to campus only to lose him to someone from the Canadian Football League, which flew him to Toronto. The Rams picked up Williams's trail again and convinced him to join several other prospects in Chicago to wait out the NFL draft.

Schuh was drafted right after the most significant pick of all time. With the second overall pick of the 1965 draft, the New York Jets took quarterback Joe Namath and signed him to a three-year, $427,000 contract. That reaffirmed the AFL's determination to fight and made the signing war so expensive that the leagues' merger became inevitable. The Jets had little trouble outbidding the St. Louis Cardinals for Namath, but wrapping up some other draft picks was not so easy. The Jets were outfoxed when they lost a second first-round pick, fullback Tom Nowatzke from Indiana. They were slow to realize that the pal who accompanied Nowatzke to New York and even sat in on contract talks was an NFL baby sitter, and he ended up delivering Nowatzke to the Lions. The Jets signed their third-round pick, Jackson State defensive end Verlon Biggs, but not before an NFL baby sitter flew him to Detroit and Washington and kept changing hotels.

The Jets almost came to blows with the Vikings before signing their seventh-round pick, defensive tackle (Diamond) Jim Harris from Utah State. Jets offensive line coach Chuck Knox and Vikings scout Joe Thomas were negotiating with Harris while sitting in separate cubicles in Utah State coach Tony Knap's offices. Harris went back and forth to negotiate, but Coach Weeb Ewbank authorized Knox to raise the stakes on the spot while Thomas had to phone Coach Norm Van Brocklin for instructions. When Knox kept quickly topping every counteroffer, Thomas accused him of eavesdropping.

"I told him," Knox wrote, "'You say that again and we're going to have the daggonedest fistfight there ever was. We're going to have it right here, in the office, not even going outside, right now.' The college coach jumped between us. The player jumped out into the hall. There wasn't any silly fight. And I later signed Jim Harris."

According to Weiss, Thomas jumped out of the stands and threw a punch at a Chargers scout trying to sign Nebraska linebacker John Kirby after the Orange Bowl on New Year's Day 1964. Kirby signed with the Vikings.

Weiss also recounted that some baby sitters were not above using blackmail. Before the 1964 draft, the story goes, a baby sitter suggested that two players, one married and the other single, get out of their hotel room and have free drinks in the lounge. There they met two women the baby sitter had hired to spend the night with the players. The baby sitter phoned the room about five o'clock in the morning to let the married player know his wife would find out about his escapade if he did not sign with the league paying his bill. The blackmailed player settled for about one-sixth of the signing bonus garnered by his roommate, who went to the other league.

And whatever became of the "provincial lad" whose two contract signings led to one of the most colorful eras in pro football history? His story is no less bizarre than any tale told in the baby sitting era. Cannon became a successful dentist in Baton Rouge, but in July 1983 he was arrested and charged in a $6 milion counterfeiting scheme. He pleaded guilty to conspiracy to possess and distribute counterfeit money and was sentenced to five years in federal prison. Released in 1986 after serving more than half his sentence, Cannon regained his dental license. But he filed for bankruptcy in 1995 and two years later was hired to run the dental clinic at the Louisiana penitentiary in Angola. Yet he has remained LSU's football hero.

Cannon was honored at the Tigers' homecoming game November 1, 1999, the fortieth anniversary of his famous punt return. As reported in the *New York Times*, "He stood on the field between the first and second quarter while his famous run played on the scoreboard. Fans stood and cheered, and players raised their helmets in salute." The LSU faithful, clearly, forgave his transgressions. Those who built the AFL probably would have forgiven them, too.

8

The Money Box

The best advice the American Football League ever got came from the enemy camp. AFL founder Lamar Hunt harbored hopes, however naive, that NFL commissioner Bert Bell might serve as the commissioner of both leagues. During the summer of 1959, Denver Broncos owner Bob Howsam was sent to run that idea by Bell at his vacation home near Atlantic City, New Jersey.

Hunt had first met Bell in 1958 when he tried to acquire an NFL franchise, and he had stayed in touch with Bell during the AFL's formative months. Bell told Howsam he could not serve as AFL commissioner, but before Howsam left, he asked Bell what he would consider the most critical issue facing the new league. Bell's reply would alter professional football's financial future: "Pool the TV money. We don't have that in the National Football League, but I'm working on it. That is a very important thing."

The AFL took Bell's advice to heart. As Howsam recalled,

> I went back and talked to Lamar and the person we would have to convince was Harry Wismer because he had that big market in New York. We decided we would get him to believe he was the one who wanted to do it, and we did. So it was

agreed we would share TV money. ABC decided to televise our games and that was what made the league. That was when we really looked at the possibility of being successful.

A half century later, television money and its equal distribution have made the NFL successful beyond its wildest dreams. The league negotiated $20 billion worth of TV contracts with four networks, not counting its own NFL Network, in multiyear deals starting in 2006. Advertisers paid the FOX Broadcasting Company $2.7 million for a thirty-second commercial spot during the telecast of the New York Giants' 17-14 victory over the New England Patriots in the 2008 Super Bowl. That game drew 97.5 million viewers, a Super Bowl record and the second-largest TV audience ever.

According to *Sports Illustrated,*

> It is television, nothing else, that has brought this ultimate gift of riches to pro football. The AFL all but leaped full-blown from the coffers of network television. The increase in franchises, the structure of the leagues, the dramatics of the playoffs and the creation of that celestial spectacle, the Super Bowl, have all been brought to us courtesy of the TV Establishment of America. Pro football, as we know it today, is plainly the son of Super Spectator.

This observation was written in 1969. Yet, it is as true today as it was then.

In November 1959 AFL owners agreed to negotiate a single TV contract for the league and equally share the rights fees, yet they did not expect a windfall. They simply wanted national exposure and the chance to survive. Of the three networks that dominated TV back then, CBS already carried most NFL games, and NBC had no interest in the new league. That left ABC, which was receptive to new programming but had no sports division and little cash. Hunt, in no position to be choosy, set his sights on ABC.

He knew that network boss Leonard Goldenson had received a loan from the Metropolitan Life Insurance Company to buy a controlling interest in ABC. So Hunt asked Harry Hagerty, a Metropolitan executive, to put in a good word with Goldenson for the AFL. After speaking with Goldenson, Hagerty advised Hunt to contact Tom Moore, ABC's president, and Edgar Scherick Jr., who produced the network's sports telecasts though his company, Sports Programs, Inc.

Hunt's timing was perfect. ABC, belittled for running a distant third in the network ratings, was picking up a major advertiser. Gillette, which targeted sports audiences to sell its razor blades, was about to switch an $8 million advertising budget from NBC to ABC. Still, Moore was only mildly interested in the AFL when he met with Hunt and Wismer. "They told me that if we would take them on, they had a chance," Moore told *Sports Illustrated*. "I told them we were interested, but I didn't think it was worth too much. We agreed to meet again."

Their next meeting was held at Wismer's New York apartment, with the Titans' owner leading the AFL's negotiations. Putting him out front proved a poor idea, even if that was the price fellow owners had to pay for Wismer's cooperation. Moore and Scherick were there on behalf of ABC, and five owners represented the AFL: Houston's Bud Adams, Los Angeles's Barron Hilton, Buffalo's Ralph Wilson, Hunt, and Wismer. Because Wismer was convinced he was being spied on, he told his visitors to arrive alone, at different times, and to cover their tracks to his apartment.

Wismer's pitch was that the AFL would present a TV-friendly game. Players' names would be stitched on the backs of their jerseys, making it easy for viewers to identify them. The league would also introduce exciting new wrinkles, notably the two-point conversion. When Moore suggested ABC might pay the AFL $800,000 year, Wismer was incensed. He angrily leaped to his feet and seemed about to storm out of his own apartment. He threw open a door, but it led to a broom closet and not an exit. Negotiations were over and so, too, perhaps was the AFL's future.

The new league regrouped, however, and resumed negotiations without Wismer. AFL commissioner Joe Foss hired Jay Michaels, a talent agent at the Music Corporation of America (MCA), to deal with ABC. (Jay's son, Al, would become the nation's top play-by-play announcer of NFL games.) MCA president David (Sonny) Werblin and Moore met over supper at the "21" restaurant in New York City in early June 1960 and agreed to a five-year, $8.5 million contract. Each of the eight AFL teams would receive more than $170,000 in the first season. That deal became the model for the NFL, too, and led Foss to observe, years later, "The relationship between professional football and television was about to change for all time."

That relationship actually had been changing since the NFL championship game on December 28, 1958. Ron Powers wrote in *Super Tube*:

> The game that made the National Football League and married it to television, a brutal poem of football, unfolded. In that bleak urban dusk, with NBC's Orthocon cameras peering spectrally into the dimness, Chris Schenkel and Chuck Thompson at the microphones and fifty million Americans watching on their black-and-white sets, the Baltimore Colts defeated the New York Giants, 23-17, at eight minutes, fifteen seconds of a sudden-death overtime.

Powers recounts that game, despite its hold on viewers, featured a production that was almost primitive. Schenkel and Thompson announced from a camera cage suspended from the upper deck in Yankee Stadium, and they were exposed to the winter elements. Cables connecting NBC cameras with the remote truck ran through the stands. Consequently, when fans began to rush toward the field during overtime, someone kicked a cable loose, and NBC temporarily lost its picture. "And in that brief span of time," Schenkel said, "one of our engineers—I wish somebody had recorded his name—actually climbed out of our cage and ran down on the field, into that mob, and found that disconnected cable and fitted it back together again."

According to *America's Game*, the technician had extra time to get the picture back on because of the antics of Stan Rotkiewicz, an NBC business manager working as a sideline statistician. As the Colts came out of a timeout and broke their huddle, Rotkiewicz ran on the field, doing a fine impression of a drunk. His smiling face and the three policemen who apprehended him were captured in a *Sports Illustrated* photograph, with the caption, "Tight Squeeze Is Put on Gay Colt Fan." NBC missed only one more play before the picture returned.

NBC held the rights to the NFL championship game. The rest of the league's television landscape was a hodgepodge. CBS or its affiliates televised regular-season games for nine teams. Bell and Scherick, then at CBS before he formed his own company, arranged the weekly regional lineup. As Scherick told Powers,

> In those days, each region of the United States had its specific advertisers—regional beers, gasolines and so forth. We'd work it out with the individual team owners. I was dealing with the Rooneys in Pittsburgh, the Bidwills and Halases in Chicago, the Maras in New York. It was great fun. Bert Bell himself ran the whole league out of his kitchen. He'd call me up every morning, just as I was soaping myself up in the shower, and we'd work out our arrangements by telephone.

By the end of the fifties, the NFL's yearly rights fees from CBS ranged from $150,000 for the Giants to $75,000 for the Green Bay Packers. NBC had a deal with the Baltimore Colts and Pittsburgh Steelers to televise one national game of the week. The Cleveland Browns, a perennial winner, had their own network. This setup was too fragmented to suit CBS. Two or three games might go head-to-head in one city, which hurt CBS's ratings and made each of those games less appealing to advertisers. CBS sports chief Bill MacPhail told the NFL owners in 1960 that he would pay $3 million a year for the entire league package; however, the bigger-market teams were in no mood to share just yet. They soon would change their minds.

Though the AFL's initial contract with ABC was modest—the NFL would sign a two-year, $9.3 million contract with CBS in 1962—each AFL team in 1960 earned more TV revenue than each of five NFL teams, including the Philadelphia Eagles, the league champions. This TV money enabled the AFL to squeeze through its difficult early years. As Powers wrote:

> The American Football League was a "studio" sport in that practically no one watched it [at least in the early years] except on television. The fact that fans showed up in stadium seats at all was a matter of mild astonishment—if not a certain inconvenience to ABC technicians, who tended to charge out on to the various fields of play, still wearing their headset phones and trailing their input cords, to berate the official for signaling the kickoff before the commercial had ended.

Still, pro football telecasts had come a long, long way in the twenty years since NBC's pioneer football production of the Brooklyn Dodgers' 23-14 victory over the Eagles on October 22, 1939, at Ebbetts Field. Attendance was only about 13,050 fans, but that could hardly be blamed on fans who stayed home to watch the game on television. Only about 500 New Yorkers viewed the game on NBC's experimental station, W2XBS. Because of its novelty and futuristic feel, this telecast was also shown in the RCA Pavilion at the World's Fair in the New York City borough of Queens.

The Ebbetts Field telecast had a crew of eight, including play-by-play announcer Allen (Skip) Walz. One camera was placed in box seats on the forty-yard line, and another camera was in the mezzanine. "I'd sit with my chin on the rail in the mezzanine, and the camera was over my shoulder," Walz said. "I did my own spotting, and when the play moved up and down the field, on punts or kickoffs, I'd point to tell the camera man what I'd be talking about." With no commercial interruptions, the game ran for only two hours, thirty-three minutes, and ten seconds. The actual telecast was even shorter. "It was a cloudy day [and] when the sun crept behind the stadium, there wasn't enough light for the cameras," Walz said. "The picture would get darker and darker, and eventually it would go completely blank, and we'd revert to a radio broadcast."

The U.S. entry into World War II stunted the growth of commercial television because TV technicians were needed for military work. After the war, NFL owners began to take notice of this curious medium. Bears owner George Halas recalled in his autobiography that in 1947, he visited *Chicago Tribune* sports editor Don Maxwell at his office and found him looking at a small black box that framed a fuzzy picture. "There it is, George," he said. "Television."

The men stared at the ten-inch screen for a few minutes, and then Maxwell asked Halas what he thought. Consider how much the football world already had changed for Halas, who in 1920 entered the Decatur Staleys, which became the Chicago Bears, in the league that became the NFL. "I don't think you could see much of a football game in a picture that small, Don," he replied. "And the pictures are so fuzzy. They remind me of the early Doug Fairbanks movies I used to see at the Bijou Nickelodeon, but those pictures were a lot bigger."

Maxwell predicted the TV image would soon become larger and clearer and, eventually, shown in color. Halas asked, skeptically, if TV would ever become more than a toy. "George, that little box will change the American way of life," Maxwell replied. "Television is coming fast. We both had better try to treat is as a friend rather than an enemy or rival. We'd better get in on the act early and try to make television go our way as much as we can."

That year, WBKB in Chicago paid Halas $900 a game to televise all six Bears' home games. "It would pay?" Halas asked. "I couldn't believe it. The money was an unexpected bonus. It did help fade the dreadful prospect, which arose now and then, of bars being packed with Bears' fans watching the Bears play in an empty stadium. I did not foresee television as a major producer of money for the Bears."

He was, of course, dead wrong. Yet Halas and his fellow owners were much more open-minded about television than their counterparts in baseball were. Big-league owners were so worried television might diminish attendance that they discouraged creative coverage. "The view a fan gets at home," said Commissioner Ford Frick, "should not be any better than that of the fan in the worst seat in the ballpark." Baseball distrusted broadcasting from the start. In 1939, the New York Giants, New York Yankees, and Brooklyn Dodgers all prohibited radio broadcasts of their home games.

The Los Angeles Rams, meanwhile, boldly accepted an offer from the Admiral Television Company to televise all their home games in 1950. To protect gate revenues, the Rams required the company to compensate them for any losses in projected ticket sales. Those losses proved substantial. The Rams' home attendance, which averaged nearly 50,000 fans in 1949, dropped by almost half. Yet when the Rams made the playoffs and a local TV blackout was restored, they drew a crowd of 83,501 fans for a 24–14 victory over the Bears. Because of that experience, Bell a year later ordered league-wide blackouts of home games. His policy was upheld in court.

NFL executives were not alone in struggling to come to grips with television. Even network decision makers seemed puzzled over how to develop the little black box's potential. "The ruling circles at CBS and NBC," Powers wrote, "were xenophobically locked into a narrow notion of television as talking radio, and were loading up the video airwaves with dozens of transplanted radio crooners, comedians and newscasters— which made for a lot of TV pictures depicting a large, smiling head in front of a spangled curtain."

It would take, consequently, network outsiders to revolutionize sports television. Scherick, who radically changed sports on the air, came from advertising. An Army meteorologist during World War II and a Harvard graduate, Scherick landed at the New York agency of Dancer Fitzgerald & Sample. His accounts included Falstaff, a St. Louis brewery that appreciated baseball's ability to sell beer. Scherick and ABC put together the Falstaff *Game of the Week* in 1953 and hired colorful announcer Dizzy Dean. The show boasted strong ratings, even though it was blacked out in all major-league cities. Two years later, Scherick hooked up Falstaff with the NFL and got a multibillion-dollar ball rolling.

It all started when Scherick received a Nebraska station's flier asking his agency to buy ads on telecasts of the Chicago Bears' and Chicago Cardinals' games. He was curious what other stations might be televising these games and found that the teams operated an eleven-station network, originating from the ABC affiliate in Chicago. It quickly dawned on Scherick that this network almost exactly covered the Falstaff distribution area, and he envisioned a partnership with Falstaff, ABC, and the NFL. Scherick told the Bears and the Cardinals that his agency, on behalf of Falstaff, would buy half their TV advertising. This campaign cost the agency about $2,000 a week, which Scherick described as "the greatest media buy in the history of television."

The Dancer agency moved Falstaff from ABC to CBS in 1956, and pro football's television profile was about to shoot up. "We got CBS into pro football," Scherick said. "They used the expertise that we had developed with the eleven-station regional network, and they brought the National Football League into the big time." The Bears, much to Halas's delight, were pulling in about $200,000 a year from radio and television.

Scherick left the Dancer agency to join CBS. He appeared in line for the top spot at CBS Sports, but he was jolted when passed over for MacPhail, the Kansas City Athletics' public relations director. By 1959, Scherick was independently producing sports for ABC. That year, Roone Arledge won an Emmy Award for producing a puppet show at NBC, but he was ambitious and eager for broader horizons. ABC was building a sports schedule and shocked the TV industry by winning the NCAA college football package for the 1960 season. Scherick hired Arledge to produce the games, and they teamed up to change TV sports forever.

Arledge held the unconventional notion that a sports telecast should be entertaining. He wrote down his concepts in a memo to Scherick that became a manifesto for producing sports on television. Arledge proposed overhauling almost every element of a sports telecast, from the audience's makeup to the technology's sophistication. For women oblivious to Xs and Os, Arledge would present pageantry. For the men, Arledge would mix shots of shapely cheerleaders with unprecedented camera angles of tackles and touchdowns.

Arledge's memo said, in part:

> Heretofore, television has done a remarkable job of bringing the game to the viewer—now we are going to take the viewer to the game. . . . We will have cameras mounted on jeeps, on mike booms, in risers or helicopters, or anything necessary to get the complete story of the game. We will use a "creepy-peepy" camera to get the impact shots that we cannot get from a fixed camera—a coach's face as a man drops a pass in the clear—a pretty cheerleader just after her hero has scored a touchdown. . . . In short—We are going to add show business to sports!

Arledge's approach would reach full bloom ten years later when, as president of ABC Sports, he would revolutionize pro football telecasts on *Monday Night Football.*

But at twenty-nine years old, Arledge, produced his first football game when Alabama played Georgia in 1960 at Birmingham's Legion Field. He told announcers Curt Gowdy and Paul Christman to develop the angle of Bear Bryant's Alabama machine versus the individual brilliance of Georgia quarterback Fran Tarkenton. Such story lines became intrinsic to Arledge's productions. Even after his death, *Monday*

Night Football producers continued to suggest a compelling story line to their announcing and camera crews in pregame production and technical meetings.

Marc Gunther and Bill Carter, in *Monday Night Mayhem*, described the young producer's debut:

> In an intimacy that was unprecedented, Arledge displayed the calm concentration of Bryant on the sideline before an important call, the youthful elation of Tarkenton after a scrambling first down, the sweet exuberance of the Alabama cheerleaders, and the anguish of a rooter with a Georgia pennant. For the first time, the television screen was filled with more than helmets and numbers colliding almost soundlessly in the distance; it was filled with emotion, the same emotion a spectator would have felt inside Legion Field. Arledge's plan had worked; he had used more microphones and more cameras in different locations to bring the feeling of the event to the spectators in their living rooms . . . Sports television was reborn that afternoon.

What Arledge did not invent, he borrowed. Videotape, which allowed for instant playback and would become integral to sports' TV, was refined for commercial use in 1959. The Ampex Corporation, a Pete Rozelle client during his public relations career, invented the technology in 1956. When Rozelle returned to the Rams as their general manager in 1957, he hired Ampex to shoot videotape of the Rams' games to help Coach Sid Gillman's game preparation. Videotape was not yet popular on TV because it required heavy machines and was hard to edit.

But ABC engineer Bob Trachinger returned from Japan with technology suitable for slow-motion videotape. Arledge jumped on the idea, and early in the 1961 season, ABC's halftime show featured the first slow-motion replay. It featured Boston College quarterback Jack Concannon's eighty-yard touchdown run against Syracuse. Editing problems prevented the replays from being shown instantaneously until Tony Verna, a CBS director, solved them in 1963. It was a happy coincidence for the NFL that innovative sports production and Commissioner Pete Rozelle took center stage at the same time. Though he was not the first NFL executive to take a keen interest in television's possibilities, nobody else in pro football ever courted and milked television as single-mindedly as did Rozelle. The NFL's partnership with television remains his legacy. Just a year after his 1960 election, Rozelle persuaded NFL owners to accept TV revenue sharing. Somewhere, Bert Bell was smiling.

Rozelle's professional background predisposed him to explore and exploit television. As the Rams' publicity director, he worked for an owner, Reeves, who had experimented with televising home games. When Rozelle left the Rams in 1955 for a public relations firm, he constantly met with New York advertising and television executives. Proximity to the major networks was a big factor in Rozelle's decision to move the NFL offices from Philadelphia to New York.

Rozelle's two-year, $9.3 million contract with CBS was only a start. For his next network deal, he called for sealed bids from the networks, starting the cutthroat competition that would continually drive up the value of the NFL package. In 1964, NBC and ABC were willing to challenge CBS' rights to NFL games. The bids exceeded even Rozelle's expectations. "The rumors were fantastic," he recalled. "I thought we might get $10 million a year." Network executives and their lawyers were ushered into Rozelle's office for the opening of bids January 24, 1964. The outer office was packed with reporters, photographers, and television crews, a sign of the media's growing fascination with sports broadcasting. Rozelle shuffled the envelopes and opened them. He first opened the NBC bid, which was $10.3 million a year, matching his high-end estimate and more than doubling the expiring CBS deal. Then Rozelle opened the ABC bid, which offered $13.2 million a year. CBS and ABC both were encouraged by a loophole in the contract that would give them the opportunity to increase advertising revenue by showing doubleheaders. Though not customarily shown, the league had not prohibited them.

Rozelle told *Sports Illustrated*:

> The ABC bid was beyond any of my dreams. Even with the doubleheader thing, I never thought it would go over $12 million a year. The CBS bid had to be an anticlimax. I opened it, and the thing was two pages long—all in fine print. The number was toward the bottom and I looked at it . . . and I looked at it again. It was for $14.1 million a year.

Scherick, then ABC's vice president in charge of programming, pointed out that his network's two-year bid of more than $26 million dwarfed the $15 million value of the entire network in 1951. Rumors were rampant, though never confirmed, that an ABC insider leaked the network's bid to CBS, enabling it to adjust the winning bid. There was, it turned out, another big winner that day. While Rozelle opened bids, the AFL waited like a gull at the docks.

NBC sports chief Carl Lindemann dejectedly walked a block back to his office after finishing third in the bidding and saw a note: "Call Joe Foss." About two hours later, Lindemann met with Foss and Werblin. Since finalizing the AFL's contract with ABC in 1960, Werblin, a close friend of NBC president Robert Kintner's, had bought the New York Jets. The AFL and NBC agreed on a five-year, $36 million deal, which took the new league off life support and into the big time. Now the AFL could fight, dollar for dollar, in the war for talent.

"The AFL's lucrative TV contract brought new prestige to the league, as well as over twenty new requests for franchises and several offers to buy existing teams," Foss said. "That year I estimated that the weakest team in the league would sell for at least $9,000,000." Back in 1960, television money bought the AFL time to survive. Four years later, TV money meant that a merger of the leagues was all but inevitable.

William Johnson wrote in *Sports Illustrated*:

The events of January 1964 meant, in the final analysis, that for better or worse, an entire sport had been bought, and it was never really going to be the same again. Everybody, including the fans, recognized—and soon accepted—that whatever pro football did in the future, the decision would have to be made in terms of the economic needs of television.

The AFL contract, in one respect, made a bigger impact on professional sports than the NFL's far richer deal. Suddenly every sports entrepreneur in America envisioned a new league that, in the AFL mold, could be sustained by television money. Within a decade, the sports landscape would include the American Basketball Association, World Hockey Association, World Football League, North American Soccer League, World Championship Tennis, and World Team Tennis. The ABA and WHA folded, though the established leagues absorbed some of their teams. Other new sports ventures went belly up or tried to reinvent themselves. Both the WCT men's tour and the NASL, interestingly, were Hunt's brainstorms. But even he could not re-create his magic from the AFL, which remains the only successful major pro sports league started in the past fifty years. Hunt caught the right waves in the right sport, and no wave was bigger than television. Subsequent new leagues failed to impress television, and that was their kiss of death.

When it came to selling television rights, Rozelle did not believe in limits. "No one I know can squeeze the last buck out of a situation the way Pete Rozelle can," said Dick Bailey, president of Hughes Sports Network. When CBS balked at renewing its contract for 1966 and 1967 at Rozelle's price, he ordered a feasibility study for the NFL to form its own network. "It was feasible for us to do it—not a great situation, but within reality," Rozelle said. "The owners voted to go along with it—we would drop CBS and start out on our own." Despite uncontested bidding, CBS agreed to pay the NFL $18.8 million a year plus $2 million a year for the NFL championship game.

It's anybody's guess whether the threat of an in-house network was more than a negotiating ploy in 1966, but the very concept provided yet more evidence of Rozelle's legendary vision. The NFL Network was launched November 4, 2003, and began televising an eight-game package in 2006. Local stations in markets of the teams playing could pick up the games; otherwise, they were usually restricted to NFL Network subscribers.

CBS assumed it had wrapped up the NFL's climactic game for $2 million a year but was in for a rude surprise once the merger was announced in 1966. Now, Rozelle was selling the Super Bowl, a much bigger game than the NFL championship. His hand was about to get even deeper into CBS' pockets. "Got a pencil handy?" Rozelle asked when he called MacPhail to quote him the price for rights to the Super Bowl. Rights for the first four Super Bowl games were sold to CBS and NBC for $9.5 million, including $1 million from each to televise the first Super Bowl in January 1967. Both networks plugged the game relentlessly, and NBC's announcers, Gowdy and Christman, made guest appearances on the *Tonight* and *Today* shows. They had come over from ABC in 1965.

Sixty million viewers watched the telecast of the Packers' 35–10 victory over the Kansas City Chiefs at the Los Angeles Memorial Coliseum. The percentage of television sets tuned to the Super Bowl, including sets not in use, were 22.6 for CBS and 18.5 for NBC. The shares, or percentage of sets in use and tuned to the game, were 43 and 36, respectively. The league broke even on a $2.8 million budget, with the networks paying most of the freight. The NFL's main disappointment was the crowd of 61,946 fans, which left some 31,000 empty seats. Attendance may have suffered because of steady media speculation that Rozelle would lift the standard blackout of games within a seventy-five-mile radius of the home stadium. When the blackout remained, it was suggested, Los Angeles fans stayed home in protest or were simply not sufficiently motivated to buy tickets at the last minute.

When the Packers kicked off to start the second half, CBS was ready, but NBC viewers were still watching a commercial. Referee Norm Schachter quickly spotted the mix-up and blew the ball dead while the kick was in the air. The Packers kicked off again to allow NBC to catch up, and league officials were relieved that the Chiefs, trailing 14–10, did not have a long kickoff return called back for television. "They told me to ask [Packers coach Vince] Lombardi to kick off again because NBC had missed the second-half kickoff," recalled Pat Summerall, a CBS reporter. "I said, 'You've got the wrong guy. I ain't doing that.'"

The first Super Bowl also marked the last time more than one major network would televise the same NFL game until December 29, 2007. The NFL Network had scheduled a game between the New England Patriots and the New York Giants, but it allowed NBC and CBS also to air the game because the Patriots were about to complete an unprecedented 16–0 regular season. This multi-network setup worked much more smoothly than the one in 1967.

The Super Bowl quickly became the nation's premier sports event. What broadcast frontier was there left for Rozelle to conquer? That would be prime time. Shortly after the New York Jets' historic upset of the Colts in the January 1969 Super Bowl, he asked the networks to consider a Monday night package. But the networks were not sure the NFL could attract viewers on a weeknight or if disrupting successful prime-time lineups would cost them money.

"We talked to CBS and they said, 'What, move Doris Day?'" Rozelle recalled. NBC was scared off when it initially agreed to televise a Monday night game, only to have its biggest star, late-night host Johnny Carson, threaten a boycott should his show be delayed for the game's finish. Only Arledge, president of ABC Sports, wanted in on the Monday night games. ABC was running third in prime-time ratings and had little to lose by showing football. Yet Arledge and Rozelle still faced a tough sell with ABC executives, who doubted they could find enough viewers, advertisers, and affiliates to make prime-time games profitable.

Rozelle once again played one network against another. He took his Monday night package to the Hughes Sports Network, which was independently owned by wealthy recluse Howard Hughes. His network was willing to let Rozelle name his price for Monday night games, and it would sell them nationally to network affiliates, including ABC's. Rozelle preferred having the games on a major network and figured ABC would cringe at the prospect of its affiliates deserting a weak prime-time lineup to buy NFL games from Hughes.

"We figured we would lose something like one hundred of our stations who would carry the game independently," Arledge said. "So it was fear, more than anything, that got the network to agree."

ABC signed a four-year deal, starting in 1970, to televise Monday Night Football. "ABC had to agree every game would be shown in color because it wasn't automatic in those days," Rozelle said. "After the first year, I felt we had a winner. I didn't necessarily feel it would last [more than] twenty years. But I was hopeful it would do very well right from the start."

Monday Night Football gave Arledge the grandest stage yet for his entertainment-driven approach to pro football. The show took the nation's viewers by storm and stayed on ABC for thirty-six years. Arledge said,

> We felt we could find a way [to present Monday night games] so we weren't dependent each week on having a barn burner, a 33-32 thriller, or a replay of a championship game to compete in prime time. The answer, of course, that we came up with was a cast of announcers different than any sports announcers that had been there before. We particularly wanted to change the role of what had been expert commentators and the way we did that was with Howard Cosell and Don Meredith.

Monday Night Football made its regular-season debut in Cleveland on September 21, 1970, and, appropriately, featured some of pro football's historic figures. Weeb Ewbank, who coached the Baltimore Colts to two NFL championships and the New York Jets to the biggest Super Bowl upset of all time, was guiding the Jets. His quarterback, Joe Namath, had both commanded a big rookie contract, which became a catalyst for merger, and personally guaranteed the Jets' Super Bowl victory over the Colts in 1969. And sitting in the ABC booth with Cosell and play-by-play announcer Keith Jackson was Meredith, once a coveted prize in the war between the leagues.

The Jets trailed 24–21 when Namath was intercepted at the New York twenty-five-yard line by linebacker Billy Andrews, whose touchdown return clinched a Browns' victory. While cameras followed Andrews and his celebrating teammates, Arledge called producer Chet Forte's attention to Namath. With his head bowed and body slumped, he was a portrait of dejection. Forte called for a camera on Namath, who remained frozen in that downcast pose, seemingly oblivious to his teammates running off the field.

That became *Monday Night Football*'s signature shot, and when Frank Gifford replaced Jackson in 1971, the most famous announcing team in sports' broadcast history was formed. Rozelle and Arledge gambled on prime-time football and won big. "I was scared to death," Cosell recalled years later. "It was a night that changed my life. We were part of a new, testing challenge and experiment in prime time on a prolonged basis."

Rozelle now had three networks televising NFL games and was enjoying a seller's market. Former NBC sports director Tom Gallery said in 1969,

> It's even worse than we think because the time on pro football games is so expensive that no one can afford more than a couple of spots. The pro football people have been pressing so hard that they are forcing sponsors right out of sight with those high fees. It's killing the networks, too, and I don't know how long it can continue.

Halas also wondered if his league's TV riches were too good to last. By the close of the 1970s, each franchise was earning about $5 million a year from television, which, Halas estimated, matched the average team's ticket revenue if it sold out all its home games. "More than one owner has awakened shuddering from a nightmare in which he saw his team playing in an empty stadium," Halas wrote. "Which is television? A bottomless pot of gold? Or a time bomb? I daily ask myself the question. Time alone can tell."

When Halas died in 1983, the pot of gold was still bottomless. Four years later, ESPN began televising Sunday night games. TNT took half the Sunday night package in 1990. As the NFL approached the fiftieth anniversary of the Greatest Game Ever Played, CBS, NBC, FOX, ESPN, and the NFL Network televised league games. For younger generations, perhaps, the 1958 title game represents no more than ancient history. For many baby boomers, though, it still evokes fond memories of when pro football was on the way up and a decade of easy living was winding down.

9

The Fifties

The Hall of Fame quarterback was waiting for the Pulitzer Prize–winning writer. Y. A. Tittle, who had played for three professional teams during a seventeen-year career, had agreed to an interview with David Halberstam, author of twenty-one books. For his next book, Halberstam was researching the 1958 NFL championship game. He and Tittle were to meet late Monday morning, April 23, 2007, at Tittle's insurance agency near Palo Alto, California.

Tittle, who did not join the New York Giants until 1961, said,

> I was confused as to why he called—I told him I was not a member of that team. He said he knew that. Lots of people, for whatever reason, have identified that as one of the greatest games every played—it had a reputation for that—and he wanted to get my perspective on the 1958 Colts . . . Johnny Unitas, Artie Donovan, and whoever else.

Tittle, while playing for the San Francisco 49ers, saw the Baltimore Colts twice in fifteen days during 1958. The Colts lost their last regular-season game, 21–12, at San Francisco on December 14, but the Colts had defeated the 49ers, 35–27, on November 30 in Baltimore. Tittle also could have told Halberstam about his special association with both Baltimore and New York. In 1948, Tittle was a rookie with the original Colts of the All-America Football Conference. He was still with them in 1950, their lone season in the NFL before they folded.

Tittle spent his prime with the 49ers but did not become a household name until he hit New York. He had lost the starting job to John Brodie, and in one of pro football's most one-sided deals ever, Tittle was traded to the Giants for guard Lou Cordileone. Tittle led the Giants to three straight NFL championship games, which made him, according to *Sports Illustrated*, "the dean of U.S. sport." He became a teammate of the Giants' stars who played in the 1958 and 1959 championship games, and in his first year he shared the quarterback job with Charlie Conerly.

Tittle's interview with Halberstam never took place. "He was on his way here when he got killed," Tittle recalled from his office. Halberstam, who won a Pulitzer Prize for his *New York Times* coverage of the Vietnam War, spoke two days earlier at the Graduate School of Journalism at the University of California, Berkeley. He had enlisted a graduate student to drive him to the interview and the car was broadsided on making a left turn. Halberstam, seventy-three, absorbed the brunt of the impact and was declared dead at the scene.

"I was sitting in the office, waiting for him to arrive," Tittle recalled. "By one o'clock, I got a call saying he'd been in an automobile accident. He was about five miles from my office—that's hitting close to home."

Why would Halberstam choose a football game for his next project? Though he's best known for such scholarly works as *The Best and the Brightest*, the story of how the United States became involved in Vietnam, Halberstam also wrote seven sports books. They include *The Breaks of the Game*, about life in the National Basketball Association in the late 1970s, and *Summer of '49*, a look back at the down-to-the-wire American League pennant race between the New York Yankees and the Boston Red Sox. At the time of his death, Halberstam had just completed *The Coldest Winter: America and the Korean War*. He had spent ten years working on that book, and his decision to write about the Greatest Game Ever Played fit his pattern of choosing subjects. "You do an allegedly serious book on politics or whatever," he said, "and then you catch your breath doing a smaller book on sports."

The impending fiftieth anniversary of the Giants-Colts' classic gave Halberstam's project timeliness. And he knew the era well. He had written *The Fifties*, a chronicle of the decade in which he graduated from high school and college. In his preface, he wrote, "The Fifties were captured in black and white, most often by still photographers; by contrast, the decade that followed was, more often than not, caught in living color on tape or film. Not surprisingly, in retrospect, the pace of the fifties seemed slower, almost languid. Social ferment, however, was beginning just beneath this placid surface."

In the fifties a storm was brewing, and when it unleashed its fury during the sixties, Americans were confused and shaken. The Eisenhower years, often referred to as the "Happy Days," are associated with an exaggerated innocence. Even Tom Brokaw, who in *The Greatest Generation* celebrated Americans who came of age in the Great Depression and World War II, acknowledged that generation also bore the warts of McCarthyism and segregation. Grace Metalious's *Peyton Place*, which by mid-1958 sold six million copies, was a metaphor for a decade that was not quite what it seemed. Metalious created a small New Hampshire town that was dull and quiet on the surface but bubbling with lust and scandal underneath.

The birth control pill, Halberstam pointed out, was developed in the fifties, yet the sixties' sexual revolution rolled in seemingly overnight. Likewise, though pro football enjoyed astonishing growth in the sixties, it was, in fact, gathering powerful momentum in the late fifties, and the 1958 championship game gave its popularity a gigantic push. Before December 28, 1958, many football fans were still convinced that the big-time colleges played the more appealing game. "Around the league this season, the pros are displaying a variety of play that college football cannot match," *Time* wrote, as if this were a revelation, in 1959. Even though CBS made a prescient move by hooking up with the NFL in the late fifties, that network's sports chief Bill MacPhail reflected: "Back then I would have preferred us to have college football because I thought the color, the rah-rah and the coeds had it all over the pros. Was I wrong!"

At the dawn of the fifties, Major League Baseball, college football, horse racing, and boxing were the nation's most popular sports. Baseball, crowned the "national pastime," was far out in front. "Baseball, more than almost anything else, seemed to symbolize a return to life in America as it had been before Pearl Harbor," Halberstam wrote in *Summer of '49.* "In the years immediately following World War II, professional baseball mesmerized the American people as it never had before and never would again."

The pecking order of big-time American sports was about to change profoundly, depending on how well each was prepared to exploit television. Professional golf took advantage of its TV exposure and the charismatic, go-for-broke star Arnold Palmer to carve out an affluent viewing audience tailor made for advertisers. Boxing lost its shine because of both its overexposure on TV and its mob associations. Horse racing started a free fall because it failed to use television to cultivate new generations of fans. U.S. sports grew up with radio, and for some, the leap to television posed too tough a challenge.

Baseball was, and still is, the ultimate radio sport. Baseball in the fifties evokes an image of a fan lazing on the porch on a hot summer day, listening to the mellow voice of Red Barber in Brooklyn or to any of the other iconic announcers whom fans came to consider part of their lives. During an era in which most fans worked nine to five and puttered around the house on weekends, folks had ample time to listen to a game that obeyed no clock. Baseball, radio, and the American lifestyle existed in perfect harmony. Radio was the king of broadcasting and baseball the king of U.S. professional sports.

At some point, however, leisure time diminished. In 1948, Dick McDonald and his brother Maurice were reinventing fast food, a sign that many Americans no longer sat down to a traditional family dinner.

Americans once flocked to movie theaters for double features, but few complained when they were charged the same admission for just one film. Baseball fans once loved their Sunday and holiday doubleheaders but do not seem to miss them much now. For those craving more action in less time, an action sport in a three-hour broadcast slot was made to order.

TV and pro football teamed up in the sixties, and sociologically minded critics saw this pairing as the consequence of a violent, fast-paced sport meshing with a violent, fast-paced decade. Ron Powers, a Pulitzer Prize–winning television critic, suggested that pro football in the sixties was "a passive accomplice to another payload of values that refuted most of the social revolution's aims." Football, in other words, was a last line of defense against the counterculture. Powers wrote in *Super Tube*:

> As seen on TV in the sixties, the National Football League leaped quickly from the status of an arcane, fringe sport to a full-blown expression of America's corporate and military ethos. It is by now commonplace to compare the pros' "bomb-blitz-penetrate" vocabulary with the argot of war, or to recall the glorification of martinet coaches such as Vince Lombardi and Don Shula, or to point out the NFL's emphasis on specialist players, one-skill drones who carried out their atomized task to robot perfection, suited the megalomaniac dreams of both corporate functionaries and vicarious warriors—including the vicarious warrior-in-chief, President Nixon, brooding on offensive plays for the Washington Redskins while real bombs blitzed and penetrated Vietnam and Cambodia, and watching a televised pro game while demonstrators chanted outside the White House. TV sports became a kind of psychic refuge for millions of Americans, a way of numbing themselves to the horrible convulsions that threatened to disintegrate society as they understood it.

Many shared this common, albeit not always so politicized, analysis of pro football's ascent during the sixties, but the sport's popularity and sociology had been percolating in the late fifties. The head-knocking rivalry between Cleveland Browns fullback Jim Brown and Giants middle linebacker Sam Huff, for instance, offered a riveting preview of where pro football was headed in the sixties and beyond.

Brown was a one-of-a-kind runner from the day he joined the Browns in 1957. He had an unprecedented combination of power, speed, and elusiveness, and many still consider him the best running back of all time. He also was among a rising tide of African American athletes who would drastically change the NFL's racial mix and force the sport to come to grips with segregation. Huff was one of the game's early television stars. Nobody raised the profile of the middle linebacker and defensive play more than he. Huff also reminded the league how much it helped business to have star players and a marquee team in New York.

Huff and Brown called attention to the *mano a mano* matchups that would help glamorize the game. Football may be the ultimate team sport, but it became personalized and star driven when fans focused on, for instance, the Colts' left tackle Jim Parker clashing with the Chicago Bears' huge and mean defensive end Doug Atkins. Game previews in print and broadcast media for the next half century would make much ado about one-on-one matchups. Brown and Huff first faced off when they were stars at Syracuse and West Virginia, respectively. Huff recalled:

> It was early in the third quarter, and here came Jim Brown through a hole, and there I was to meet him. I hit that big sucker head on, and my headgear snapped down and cut my nose, and my teeth hit together so hard the enamel popped off. He broke my nose, broke my teeth, and knocked me cold. I woke up in the training room with an ice pack on my head and my nose bleeding.

Huff had a better day when the Browns and Giants met in a 1958 playoff game at Yankee Stadium, the winner of which would play the Colts for the NFL championship. The Giants tied the Browns for first place in the Eastern Conference by beating them 13–10 on the last day of the regular season. The playoff game, too, was a defensive duel. Coach Paul Brown, despite boasting a Hall of Fame backfield with Brown and Bobby Mitchell, tried to beat the Giants by throwing. Brown, who rushed for a league-record 1,527 yards in 1959, carried just seven times for eight yards, and the Giants won 10–0. The only touchdown was scored in the first quarter on a trick play. From the Cleveland eighteen-yard line, Conerly handed off to halfback Alex Webster, who gave the ball to halfback Frank Gifford on a reverse. After picking up eight yards, Gifford lateraled to Conerly, who scored. Without that play, or with a more balanced attack by the Browns, there might not have been the Greatest Game Ever Played. Or it may have been played without the Giants.

The Colts' 23–17 victory in sudden-death overtime made Unitas the nation's number one football hero. Yet, the Giants—and especially their defense—saw their popularity rise even in defeat. As the Giants moved toward a title-game rematch with the Colts in 1959, Huff was featured on the cover of *Time* under the banner "Pro Football: Brawn, Brains & Profits." Such exposure represented huge strides for a sport that began the decade on the fringes. According to *Time*:

> Sunday after Sunday, pro quarterbacks have learned that whatever play they call, Huff is likely to be in front of it. Sam Huff is strong enough to flatten a plunging fullback such as the Chicago Bears' Rick Casares, swift enough to recover from a block in time to nail a halfback sprinting around end, smart enough to diagnose pass patterns and throw an offensive end off stride with an artful shoulder. But Huff is at his rugged best when he knifes through the line and "red-dogs" a quarterback as he fades to pass.

Pro football was closing in on baseball for bragging rights as the national pastime. The game was acquiring a critical, secondary audience. Every sport can claim a hardcore following, but that alone does not feed networks and advertisers. Those kingmakers of sport demand access to hordes of stay-at-home listeners and viewers. And the quickest way to lure more fans is to give them heroes. Stars like Unitas, Brown, and Huff were making a place in America's sporting consciousness and vernacular. Even pre-teenagers knew about the "red dog," or blitz. Moreover, those precocious fans would help the sport thrive into the next millennium.

"The crush of Huff's tackle can stir the Giant bench to a bellowing glee," *Time* went on, "set the rabid fans in Yankee Stadium to rumbling out on their own rapid-fire cheer like the chugging of a steam engine: 'Huff-Huff-Huff-Huff-Huff.' When Sam is on the field, the toughest fans in the U.S.'s toughest sport see what they came to see." Even before the sixties arrived, pro football was indeed building its image as a sport of brawn, brains, and profits.

Time continued,

> As thousands of fans are happily discovering, pro football is a game of precise and powerful virtuosity—incredible catches, runners who break away from swarms of opponents just when they seem stopped, crunching tackles and jet-powered blocks. No experienced pro fan leaves a game in its last five minutes when his team is only two touchdowns behind—any club can, and may, explode in those five minutes and win. Pro football is a game in which every carefully selected, battle-tried man seems larger than life, not only in skill and speed, but in sheer brute strength.

About a month after that cover story, on December 27, 1959, the Giants faced the Colts in Baltimore for the NFL title. The rematch did not recapture the drama of the previous year. "The city was ablaze with excitement," wrote John Steadman in the *Baltimore Sun*. "Hopes were high. A momentous moment had arrived." But the Giants absorbed a twenty-four-point steamrolling in the fourth quarter, and the Colts won 31–16. Colts center Buzz Nutter tied up Huff for most of the afternoon, and pregame comparisons with the 1958 game proved moot. "That game will live for the ages," Steadman wrote in 1999. "The second meeting is almost forgotten."

Not so the winning quarterback. Unitas's guts and golden arm struck a chord with sports fans. So did his rags-to-riches story. Released by the Pittsburgh Steelers in 1955, he played semipro football for $6 a game before getting a tryout with the Colts a year later. Then, with a second straight heroic performance in the NFL's showcase game, John Unitas became pro football's Joe DiMaggio, an understated and classy champion. Given his stoop-shouldered gait, Unitas did not match DiMaggio's elegant grace, but Unitas did not play an elegant or graceful game. He was easily recognized by his crew cut, black high-top shoes, and willingness to buy time for his receivers to get open.

Colts wide receiver Raymond Berry recalled,

He'd wait in the pocket until the absolute last second, deliver the ball right on the money, and get smashed in the mouth. Then he'd call the same play again and hold the ball a little longer and get smashed in the mouth even harder. The bridge of his nose would be split. His mouth would be full of blood. Do you think he cared? John would have been a great middle linebacker.

During the Colts' championship seasons, Unitas was building a series of forty-seven straight games with at least one touchdown pass. This record is pro football's equivalent of DiMaggio's remarkable fifty-six-game hitting streak. Near the end of Unitas's streak, in 1960, Atkins, who got past Parker and was doing whatever it took to preserve a 20–17 lead in Chicago, bashed Unitas's nose into a bloody mess. "The ref stuck his head in the huddle and said, 'Take all the time you need,'" Nutter, the center, recalled. "You know what John said to him? He said, 'Get the hell out of here so I can call the play.'" Unitas dropped back from the Bears' forty-yard line and hit halfback Lenny Moore down the right sideline for a touchdown and a 24–20 victory.

NFL stars now were getting their stories told and enjoying more or less equal billing with big-league baseball stars. Yankee Stadium proved big enough for both sports. With the Yankees playing in nine World Series from 1949 to 1958 and the Giants in three NFL title games from 1956 to 1959, New York was loaded with future Hall of Fame players and championship teams. The Giants used the Yankees' clubhouse, and Huff won't ever forget that he and centerfielder Mickey Mantle shared a locker.

As Huff said,

> It's just unbelievable when you look back at it to have had Tom Landry coaching defense and Vince Lombardi coaching offense, and being around Kyle Rote and Frank Gifford—the glamour guys—and Pat Summerall. The Yankees were always in the World Series and we had to play our first three games away and practice at Fordham University. We all stayed at the Concourse Plaza Hotel, up the street from Yankee Stadium. We all went to Toots Shor's [restaurant in Manhattan] because Toots never charged us. That was a great time to be a player. That really was a golden age of sports.

In 1960, Huff agreed to wear a microphone during training camp and exhibition games for a CBS documentary, *The Violent World of Sam Huff*. With that telecast, which Walter Cronkite narrated, middle linebackers became headliners. "We were almost like offensive guards, which is what I came up as," Huff recalled. "We were just there. The stars were the offensive people, like Charlie Conerly."

Giants fans began chanting for the defense in 1956, and that side of the ball truly got noticed when a CBS microphone was run under

Huff's arm and taped to the front of his shoulder pads. The resulting footage captured the speed and smack of pro football and the middle linebacker's role at the intersection of mayhem. "I did not like the title, but it was catchy," said Huff, who during eight years with the Giants played in six championship games.

> Football is a violent game, but it's controlled, too. War is violent, and I guess football is war without guns.
>
> When they said, "You're going to be wired for sound," I said, "What? You've got to be kidding. A microphone?" I did not realize what carrying an extra pound around would mean. I played all the defense and on the punt return team and kickoff team. I was very seldom out of the game. In practice and preseason, that one pound got a little heavy. We were playing the Bears up in Toronto and they had a wide receiver actually come and hit me after the play. I kind of knocked him down and said, "What are you doing?" He said, "I know if I hit you, I'm gonna get on TV." I got a grand total of five hundred dollars for doing it and the rights to a rental car. I was the only one in camp who had a car. But I never got to use it. Everybody wanted to borrow it.

Using live microphones and candid footage would become integral to the game's presentation. NFL Films would take viewers to the sideline, on the playing field, and behind locker-room doors, providing unprecedented perspectives of Sunday afternoons. And as the Giants happily discovered, a winning team in the big city brought the advertisers running. Gifford, the handsome halfback, pitched Vitalis hair tonic on television and in newspaper ads. Cliff Livingston, though the least known of the Giants' linebackers, was hired for a TV ad during the 1958 season. Conerly was an early Marlboro Man, one of the most famous advertising figures in the history of Madison Avenue.

Profitable relationships developed in the fifties between pro football, Madison Avenue, and the networks. Former Dallas Cowboys president Tex Schramm recalled in his biography,

> The Fifties was a decade in which everybody became watchers instead of doers. This was personified by the television sets that took over our dens and our living rooms. Television meant the end of minor league baseball as we had known it and also minor league entertainment. Why pay to see a stage show with one big name and no other major talent, when you could turn on your TV and watch the best entertainers in the world? I think this also signaled the end of regionalism. People started thinking more on a national scale.

The Marlboro Man represented Philip Morris, one of the nation's biggest advertisers. Jack Landry, the company's head of marketing, was instrumental in putting pro athletes in commercials and was NFL commissioner Pete Rozelle's best friend in New York. Landry actually became one of the NFL's baby-sitters, and recruited others, during the signing war with the American Football League. Landry also used his marketing contacts and experience to help Rozelle turn the Super Bowl into the nation's biggest corporate picnic.

The decade of the fifties, Halberstam wrote, "revolutionized Madison Avenue." Radio advertising was swallowed by television. "We discovered that this was no tame kitten; we had a ferocious man-eating tiger," said Rosser Reeves, an advertising executive who changed the face of political campaigns by producing ads for Dwight Eisenhower during the 1952 presidential race. "We could take the same advertising campaign from print or radio and put it on TV, and even when there were very few sets, sales would go through the roof." BBD&O, an agency that favored television early, saw its billings jump from $40 million in 1945 to $235 million in 1960.

Pro football and advertising, booming in the same era, were natural partners. Big tobacco, pressured by reports that were starting to connect cigarettes with cancer, tried to satisfy smokers' health concerns by introducing filter-tip cigarettes. Philip Morris' filter-tip brand was Marlboro, originally marketed to women. Landry hired the Leo Burnett Agency in Chicago to make his filter-tip cigarettes appealing to men, and the upshot was the Marlboro Man. The agency prepared ads with rugged-looking male smokers, including the cowboy who became the campaign's signature figure. Though Conerly's role in the campaign was short lived, here was a quarterback in New York making ads years before Joe Namath hit town.

The pro athletes making commercials in the fifties had one thing in common—they all were white. Though the Los Angeles Rams in 1946 made Kenny Washington and Woody Strode the first African American players of the NFL's modern era, the floodgates did not open quickly for other African American players. The *Pro Football Chronicle* calculated that in 1950, NFL rosters included only eighteen African American players, or 4 percent of the league. By 1959, the total was only fifty-two players, or 11.5 percent of the league. Washington Redskins owner George Preston Marshall fought against integrating his roster, partly because his team's regional television audience was largest in the South. "We'll start signing Negroes when the Harlem Globetrotters start signing whites," Marshall said.

Not even the prospect of fielding a winner, a driving force of integration for many pro and college teams, could budge Marshall. Finally, President John Kennedy's secretary of the interior, Stewart Udall, warned the owner that he could be held in violation of federal law when the Redskins began playing at D.C. Stadium in 1961. It was technically a government facility, and in it, discrimination was illegal. Marshall finally was given a year's grace. He promised to integrate his team in 1962 and acquired Mitchell from the Browns.

If Marshall was not influenced after Jim Brown steamrolled his defense, other owners were. To ignore African American players was to invite haplessness, and the Redskins experienced one-win seasons in 1960 and 1961. As the AFL organized in 1959, competition for top players meant that neither league could afford to bypass the best African American prospects. The Texans' first star was Abner Haynes, an African American running back from North Texas State. Hunt's franchise scouted the historically black colleges, especially after his team moved to Kansas City, and signed such standouts as wide receiver Otis Taylor and defensive tackle Buck Buchanan. No team, however, could find another Jim Brown.

Time reported in 1959,

> Not since the 1930s, when Bronko Nagurski was crumpling lines for the Chicago Bears, have football fans seen such a numbing fullback as the Cleveland Browns' young Jimmy Brown. Magnificently muscled, Brown has a sprinter's speed, strength enough to carry along a brace of tacklers. When he hits defensive backs with a low shoulder, he can send them cartwheeling.

Furthermore, though Brown was not yet the social activist he would become, he represented a generation of African American athletes who would not stand for the slurs and second-class treatment their predecessors were asked to tolerate just to get their feet in the door.

Pro football executives began to realize their sport and segregation were incompatible, particularly as both leagues expanded to Deep South cities, where Jim Crow laws remained. The NFL and AFL were expanding to Texas in 1960, and New Orleans and Atlanta were among the prime candidates for new franchises. Both leagues knew they would constantly be embarrassed unless they discouraged second-class treatment of African American players. When Syracuse played Texas Christian in the January 1957 Cotton Bowl, Brown was not allowed to stay at the team's hotel in Dallas and was shuttled off to Fort Worth.

Curtis McClinton, a star running back at the University of Kansas, was not welcome at a Houston hotel when his team played Rice in the 1961 Bluebonnet Bowl. Kansas coach Jack Mitchell claimed that McClinton was a Native American, which was partly accurate, and kept him out of sight. McClinton recalled,

> When I got off the bus, one of the trainers said, "Come here, Curtis, we need to talk to you." We went through the side door, where they had my room. When it was time for me to leave, they came and got me. I had no idea what that scenario was all about. They wanted to make sure there wasn't a litmus test.

McClinton, a proficient pianist and vocalist, also was puzzled when Mitchell told him a music professor was going to take him to dinner. "I had a ball," McClinton said. "But I was oblivious to the fact that this was the alternative because I couldn't eat with the team. Nor could I check in with the team. They slipped me through."

Amid this racial divide, Schramm organized the Cowboys in 1959. As the Rams' publicity director, he had visited Dallas in 1948 to promote an exhibition game against the Philadelphia Eagles and found plenty of media interest in quarterback Bob Waterfield and his actress wife, Jane Russell. But when Schramm handed a photo of Kenny Washington to sports staffers at local newspapers, they would pass it around and chuckle. "No, I don't think they were bigots during those times," Schramm said. "They'd just never been exposed to the black player before."

Schramm told Dallas civic leaders that he could not run a successful NFL franchise if any visiting players faced discrimination. That behavior, he said, would embarrass both the city and team. The Citizens Council, comprised of corporate leaders, already had organized a biracial committee to meet with the National Association for the Advancement of Colored People (NAACP) president Roy Wilkins to prepare Dallas for school integration in 1961.

Schramm, however, needed hotel integration in 1960, and Dallas hotels would have preferred to delay the inevitable. A Ramada Inn with Phoenix-based management agreed to integrate as long as other hotels in Dallas promised not to stir up animosity. Partly at Schramm's insistence, the Cotton Bowl in 1960 also eliminated a separate seating section for African Americans at pro football games.

Neither Dallas pro team had a strong African American presence at first. Yet McClinton, AFL Rookie of the Year for the Texans in 1962, credits Hunt for promoting tolerance.

> He cultivated in the basket of blatant racism and segregation, in his hometown, a power to change professional football. All these people in the NFL, all these easterners, knew not one damn thing about the ethics and morality of a sport that represented manhood. Lamar goes beyond the American Football League and sports. Lamar goes to a cultural and economic transition for the South and America.

The AFL's ugliest racial incident, oddly, did not involve a franchise city. The league All-Star Game was scheduled for January 16, 1965, in New Orleans, one of several cities interested in acquiring an AFL expansion team. A week before the game, however, twenty-one African American players complained to Commissioner Joe Foss about discrimination they faced in New Orleans. "Taxi drivers and café owners were giving them a bad time," he said. "Cabbies would drive them out to the boondocks, take their money, and speed off, leaving them stranded. Or they'd go into some café in the French Quarter, hang their coats up, and somebody would take them off the hook and throw them on the floor." Foss asked the players to stay calm and not retaliate. But their shabby treatment continued.

"Finally, I sent word, 'We're moving,'" Foss recalled. "It was less than a week before the game, but there was no way I was going to have my players subjected to that kind of crap. I just said, 'Adios,' and moved the All-Star Game to Houston." The abrupt move, not surprisingly, hurt attendance at Jeppesen Stadium, the Oilers' original home. A crowd of only 15,446 watched the West defeat the East 38–14. San Diego fullback Keith Lincoln and Denver cornerback Willie Brown were voted the most outstanding offensive and defensive players.

Harsh discrimination was not confined to the South, as African American players realized when the Texans moved to Kansas City in 1963. McClinton, despite having signed a six-figure contract, lived in a basement apartment because he could not find housing outside the central city. He recalled,

> I was more than well compensated, but I was a "niggah." I was a black boy. It was a better interracial situation in Dallas because of the masses [of black citizens] and Bishop, the black university. That was another dynamic you played with, in regards to personal insult and slights. Whether or not somebody called you a "niggah," you were treated as such. You may have been called "black boy" before you walked into the stadium. That pressure doesn't exist today.

African Americans were not the only players hungry for better opportunities in pro football as the fifties ended. Because the NFL was standing pat with just a dozen teams, there were jobs for only 432 players plus replacements for those injured. The supply far exceeded the demand. Given the yearly exodus of players from college campuses and the rapid turnover of college and pro coaching staffs, the pool of players and coaches has remained almost bottomless. Without competition, the NFL could control its roster sizes and player salaries. That closed shop was turned upside down when the AFL came along.

Players who languished on NFL benches, or had been released, received second chances in the AFL. The new league's early star quarterbacks were NFL castoffs. Four of them accounted for the first five AFL championships: George Blanda in Houston, Len Dawson in Dallas,

Tobin Rote in San Diego, and Jack Kemp in Buffalo. Kemp offered a classic case of a worthy player denied an opportunity by a virtual monopoly. Picked by the Detroit Lions in the seventeenth round of the 1957 draft, he was cut during the preseason. In 1958, Kemp briefly made the Giants' roster, along with wide receiver Don Maynard, who became a Hall of Famer in the AFL.

The Giants suggested Kemp get some experience in the Canadian Football League in 1959. He was cut early in the season, and the 49ers signed him for their taxi squad. Kemp was activated after Tittle was injured, but Paul Brown prevented Kemp from playing. Brown complained to NFL commissioner Bert Bell that Kemp was violating a rule against playing in the CFL and the NFL in the same year. Kemp was eager to try the new league, especially because his first AFL salary, $11,500, was more than he would have earned in the NFL. He signed with the Los Angeles Chargers, and in 1964 he led the Buffalo Bills to the AFL championship.

Dawson, a Hall of Fame quarterback, was another first-rate player who fell victim to a buyer's market. The Steelers' first-round draft choice in 1957, Dawson sat on the bench for three years behind Earl Morrall and then behind Bobby Layne. The 1959 season found him itching to get out of Pittsburgh, and he was traded to Cleveland, only to sit two years behind Milt Plum. "I never learned anything about the quarterback position," Dawson recalled. "I never had a quarterback coach. They couldn't tell you anything about techniques, footwork, all that stuff. Bobby Layne was a great competitor but his fundamentals were terrible. My skills eroded. Paul Brown was a terrific organizational coach, but he didn't know anything about the quarterback position."

Brown granted Dawson his release in 1962, allowing him to sign with the Texans. His new coach, Hank Stram, had been an offensive coach at Purdue while Dawson led the Big Ten in passing and total offense. "As soon as he saw me, he could see, 'My god, what happened to this guy?'" Dawson recalled. "That was my savior. I just wanted an opportunity. You can't be a competitor if you don't get the chance to compete."

Dawson played in the first Super Bowl and later led the Chiefs to a victory over the Minnesota Vikings in the fourth Super Bowl. He might have remained merely an obscure NFL reserve had not Hunt been inspired to form his own league. Brainstorms of the fifties became breakthroughs in the sixties, whether in politics, race relations, sex, science, or sports.

Reviewing Halberstam's book, *The Fifties*, the *Christian Science Monitor* wrote: "Events and key personalities during the '50s not only made the revolutionary '60s happen, they were as full of ground-breaking episodes as any decade in 20th-century American history." The NFL, too, had a transitional figure who revolutionized the league in the 1960s. He, of course, was Pete Rozelle.

10

Visionary

Pete Rozelle was minding his own business, and the business of the Los Angeles Rams, when he went to Miami Beach in January 1960 for the NFL's annual winter meeting. Heading the agenda were the election of a commissioner to replace the late Bert Bell and the consideration of expansion to Dallas and Minneapolis. None of this concerned Rozelle, or so he thought.

Thirty-three years old, Rozelle was the Rams' bright, young, and universally liked general manager. In a league filled with cliques and animosity, his popularity made him an anomaly. On January 26, 1960, at the end of a bitter and exhausting seven-day, twenty-three-ballot ordeal, Rozelle was elected the third commissioner in NFL history. "I may have been picked because I was the only one who hadn't alienated most of the people at the meeting," he said. Rozelle was right, as he usually would be during his twenty-nine years in office.

With hindsight, it's easy to assume that NFL owners identified Rozelle as a wunderkind who would lead them into a gold-plated future. The owners, in fact, were hopelessly divided. They seemed as rudderless and uncooperative as they were before Bell took over in 1946. He and his stabilizing influence had passed away October 11, 1959.

NFL owners stumbled into an inspired choice. The NFL would

grow into America's premier sports league under Rozelle's leadership. When he announced his retirement on March 22, 1989, the league had grown from thirteen teams in 1960 to twenty-eight. Average attendance for regular-season games increased from 40,106 to 60,446 fans. Each team's annual television revenues climbed from $330,000 in 1962, when the first league-wide package was signed, to almost $17 million. The Super Bowl just before Rozelle's retirement, the San Francisco 49ers' 20-16 victory over the Cincinnati Bengals, drew 110.78 million viewers. It was the sixth most highly rated television program ever.

Yet old-guard owners wanted a continuation of the Bell regime, which led them to support Austin Gunsel, a former Federal Bureau of Investigation agent and NFL treasurer who became acting commissioner upon Bell's death. Newer owners, however, wanted fresh leadership. Rams owner Dan Reeves predicted after Rozelle's election:

> I think you will find a new group in power in the league from now on. Newer, younger leadership is exerting itself. The "old guard" is losing its control on the league and the power is moving to the west. This league has for many years been dominated by [Chicago's] George Halas and [Washington's] George Preston Marshall to a lesser degree. This is a complete reversal of form.

In truth, Halas did not care who was elected but kept abstaining, ballot after ballot. The point man on expansion, he was focused solely on adding two franchises. The votes for a commissioner broke down into two factions, and Halas feared his endorsement of any candidate would alienate at least one of the nine owners he needed to approve expansion. Halas had struggled to gain any support for expansion until the American Football League came along, and he was not about to blow this long-awaited opportunity. To elect a commissioner or approve expansion, a three-quarters' majority of all votes cast was required.

Gunsel and San Francisco 49ers attorney Marshall Leahy were the only candidates when voting began Wednesday, January 20, at the Kenilworth Hotel. Despite the support generated by his close association with Bell, Gunsel lacked Bell's take-charge personality and his candidacy ran out of steam. Leahy, however, was more forceful and represented the league's young blood. Sponsored by 49ers owners Vic Morabito and Tony Morabito, Leahy was almost elected on the second ballot. He outpolled Gunsel, eight votes to three. Halas abstained, leaving Leahy a vote shy of a three-quarters' majority.

According to the Rams and 49ers, Halas reneged on a promise that if Leahy could muster eight votes, Halas would cast the clincher. Reeves said,

> He had guaranteed Vic Morabito that he would vote for Leahy as soon as Leahy had eight other votes. It got to that point three times. Each time, Halas went back on his word and still refused to cast the vote that would have elected Leahy. Halas felt the vote on the commissioner might upset the balance on expansion and he considered expansion the more important of the two subjects.

Halas's strategy turned the election into a marathon. He viewed expansion, which was next on the agenda, as a weapon to kill the AFL and rid himself of the hapless Chicago Cardinals. The Cardinals and Bears alternated home dates, and because of the league's local TV blackout policy, the Bears' road games were not televised in Chicago. This situation was costly to both Halas and CBS, which televised the Bears' games. The Cardinals had flirted with moving, and Halas suspected they finally would leave once expansion began. Though Cardinals owners Walter and Violet Wolfner had no interest in moving to Dallas or Minneapolis, the start of expansion might force them to grab the most desirable open market while they still had the chance.

Violet Wolfner, representing the Cardinals in Miami Beach, opposed expansion. So did Marshall, who did not want to share his profits or regional television audience. Giants co-owner Wellington Mara also seemed cool to expansion, so Halas could not afford to lose any other votes. Tex Maule wrote in *Sports Illustrated*,

> He cared very little about who would be elected commissioner, and he sat quietly through the long drawn-out arguments. During the recesses and frequent caucuses among small groups of owners, he plugged away for expansion, shoring up his certain votes and trying to secure a commitment from the only uncertain team, the New York Giants. While Halas was fighting his undercover war for expansion, the rest of the owners were haggling over the selection of a commissioner. Halas never voted. He sat quietly in the meeting, passing when the vote came to him. He had expansion votes on both sides of the commissioner question—everyone but Marshall on the anti-Leahy faction, everyone but [Jack and Wellington] Mara and Wolfner on the Leahy side. He did not want to offend any of his supporters and he took no sides.

Halas's worries were well founded. According to *America's Game*, when Halas was asked to secure Leahy's election on the second ballot, Baltimore Colts owner Carroll Rosenbloom warned, "George, if you vote for Leahy, you can forget about expansion."

Rosenbloom, Marshall, and the Philadelphia Eagles' Frank McNamee backed Gunsel. They wanted the league office to remain in Philadelphia because it was convenient for them, and they considered Gunsel a sympathetic ear. Pittsburgh Steelers owner Art Rooney joined them in later rounds. The other owners, except Halas, stuck with Leahy, though he insisted on being allowed to run the league from San Francisco. That position ultimately cost him the election. "I think he would have been an excellent commissioner," Cleveland Browns coach and owner Paul Brown said. "He was an impressive man and had the support to be elected. But he wouldn't move from San Francisco. I think if you really want something, you don't give too much thought to where you're living."

After four days of stalemate, Leahy checked out of the Kenilworth and remained a candidate in absentia. Gunsel's candidacy began fading, and old-guard voters looked elsewhere. McNamee asked Brown to take the job, but he refused. Detroit Lions president Edwin J. Anderson and Colts general manager Don Kellett also were proposed. When Kellett was rejected, his boss, Rosenbloom, became angry. "You people are being ridiculous," he fumed. "You don't want to compromise. If God Almighty came down from heaven and agreed to serve as commissioner, you'd vote for Leahy."

Finally, on January 26, Brown and the Maras concluded Leahy was unelectable. They drew up a new list of candidates that included Rozelle but was topped by Packers coach and general manager Vince Lombardi. Green Bay president Dominic Olejniczak would not allow that, which left Rozelle as the most logical choice. During a recess, Brown and the Maras asked Reeves if he would allow them to nominate Rozelle. He agreed, but because the Rams' ownership was divided, Rozelle and Reeves phoned part owners Fred Levy Jr. and Ed Pauley for their permission. "They were as amazed as I was," Rozelle said. "When they gave me their blessing, I turned the telephone to Dan so he could explain the background of how it happened I was being considered."

Now Rozelle's supporters had to forge a three-quarters' majority. Wellington Mara lobbied Rooney, who told McNamee that the pro-Leahy group was willing to switch to Rozelle. "Who the hell is Pete Rozelle?" McNamee asked. His West Coast ties made him acceptable to the Leahy bloc. For the old guard, he had the posthumous blessing of Bell, who had interceded with feuding Rams owners in 1957 and picked Rozelle as their general manager. Rozelle interviewed with the twelve owners and then was asked to leave while they discussed his candidacy and voted for the twenty-third time. Reporters barely noticed Rozelle waiting in the men's room, washing his hands when anyone walked in. Rosenbloom nominated Rozelle, and the stalemate soon ended. Rozelle was called back in the room and told he had been elected. "I can honestly say," he cracked, "I come to you with clean hands."

Rozelle received eight of nine votes cast. The 49ers decided they were morally obliged to stick with Leahy. The Lions, Rams, and Bears abstained—the Rams because they had a conflict of interest with Rozelle working for them and Halas because of his expansion agenda. It was not clear why the Lions abstained. "They finally picked Pete as a compromise because both sides thought they could control him," said longtime Dallas Cowboys president Tex Schramm. "But they were wrong. Pete was a lot stronger than any of them realized."

Rozelle quickly showed the public relations skills he had polished in the corporate world. He said,

> To say that filling the shoes of the late Bert Bell as commissioner is a challenge would be a gross understatement. No one will ever fill his shoes. I never was so surprised in my life when I learned I was being considered. Up to now the steps forward in my career have followed in orderly fashion. This is beyond my comprehension. I never thought it would happen. When I first heard my name being mentioned, I could only think that it was a great honor to be considered, but I never dared believe I would be elected.

That same day, AFL cofounder Lamar Hunt was named league president. A day later, January 27, Minneapolis withdrew from the AFL, though its intentions were known since November. The AFL replaced Minneapolis with Oakland on January 28. This alignment marked the deployment of forces for a bitter and costly war.

There would be no honeymoon for Rozelle. As commissioner, his immediate order of business was expansion. During Bell's funeral, Halas asked his fellow owners which new markets they favored, and

Dallas and Minneapolis emerged as top choices. Clint Murchison Jr.'s franchise in Dallas would aim a dagger at the throat of Hunt's Texans, and Halas promised the Minneapolis group an NFL franchise in return for deserting the AFL.

Rozelle said upon his election,

> I am in favor of expansion, just as Mister Bell was, and I think every member of the league is, too, in some form or other. Just how it will come and when is a question that I cannot answer. The great growth of interest in professional football has created a heavy demand for membership in several population centers.

Expansion, in fact, became official two days later. Murchison, partner Bedford Wynne, and Schramm were stuck in Miami Beach, waiting out the election to get a vote on their franchise application. Their wait was rewarded when Dallas became the NFL's thirteenth franchise. Halas secured ten votes, with opposition only from Marshall and the Wolfners, who moved the Cardinals to St. Louis in March. Dallas would play each of the other twelve teams once in 1960. Minnesota also was admitted and would start play in 1961. The AFL, predictably, was outraged.

"This is an act of war," Commissioner Joe Foss said. "We will go to court or Congress to prevent the NFL from putting the AFL franchise in Dallas out of business. You have antitrust laws to take care of such situations."

Rozelle shot back, "They moved into our territory in New York and in Los Angeles and in San Francisco. Why shouldn't we be allowed to move into Dallas?"

Hunt replied, "It's not the same at all. In our case, it's just like a little dog going into the big backyard of a big dog. But in their case it's the big dog going into the little backyard and asking the little bitty dog if there's not room for him. It's the size of the backyard that counts."

Rozelle quickly found his new job to be one of handling constant crises. Just three months after his election, he was a central figure in the Rams' lawsuit to prevent Heisman Trophy winner Billy Cannon from signing with the AFL's Houston Oilers. The suit proved embarrassing to Rozelle because it revealed that, when he was the Rams' general manager, he had signed Cannon before his college eligibility expired. A federal judge agreed with Cannon's lawyers that Rozelle had taken advantage of the player's supposed lack of business experience.

Rozelle had better luck initiating a league-wide television agreement, which would become his legacy. Bell had been a voice in the wilderness for equally sharing TV revenues among NFL owners and, ironically, influenced AFL owners to adopt such a plan in 1959. NFL owners preferred cutting their own TV deals. Nine teams were tied to CBS or its affiliates, and in 1960 that network offered to televise a lucrative league-wide package. Owners still were not receptive, but a year later, at the winter meeting in New York, Rozelle told them: "Much of the past year has been spent in developing a television plan for the future. The NFL has been credited with harnessing television and using it to greater advantage than any other sports activity. This position, however, will be lost without planning for the future."

As AFL owners had realized, approval of revenue sharing was unlikely without cooperation from New York. As owners in the nation's dominant television market, the Maras would be asked to concede a financial and competitive advantage. Wellington Mara's speech in favor of sharing TV money helped put him in the Pro Football Hall of Fame in 1997, but he acknowledged it was his brother, Jack, who brought him around to that position. "We should all share, I guess," Wellington Mara told his fellow owners. "Or we're going to lose some of the smaller teams down the line, and we've all stuck together."

Rozelle signed a two-year, $9.3 million TV deal with CBS in April 1961, the first of his many broadcast coups. Yet it collapsed two months later. Though the AFL's first TV deal went unchallenged, the NFL encountered federal opposition when a court ruled that its TV contract violated antitrust law. Rozelle lobbied Congress and acquired a limited antitrust exemption that allowed each league to negotiate a single TV package. Rozelle then reinstated the original CBS contract, effective in 1962. The AFL already had a five-year deal with ABC, and pro football had the map to the broadcast treasure that would grow continually for the next fifty years.

Foss and Rozelle briefly buried the hatchet during a four-hour meeting at the St. Louis airport two weeks after Rozelle's election. They agreed that neither would tamper with players under contract in the other league. Rozelle publicly praised Foss after their meeting, but they did not trust each other. Foss announced a month later that he was asking the Department of Justice to take antitrust action against the NFL.

Foss cited the NFL for dissuading owners from joining the AFL by promising them NFL franchises, for putting a competing franchise in Dallas solely to damage the AFL, for threatening players with blacklisting and trying to get them to break contracts, and for interfering with the AFL's television contract and allegedly reducing its value. The AFL filed an unsuccessful $10 million lawsuit against the NFL that came to a head in May 1962. Rozelle was relieved to win that case, yet keeping his own house in order was no picnic, either.

The Green Bay Packers had just won the 1962 championship when Rozelle asked FBI agents to investigate reports that NFL players, particularly Packers star Paul Hornung, associated with gamblers and bet on league games. Rozelle had visited each team the previous summer and warned players that betting would be severely punished, possibly with expulsion from the NFL. Hornung had befriended Bernard (Barney) Shapiro, a Las Vegas hotel and gambling figure who placed legal bets in Las Vegas on NFL games. He phoned Hornung each week for his opinion on the Packers' chances, and Hornung eventually asked Shapiro to make bets for him on college and pro games. There was no evidence that Hornung bet against the Packers.

Shortly after the title game, Rozelle called Hornung to New York and asked him to take a lie detector test to answer questions about his alleged betting. Hornung refused to take the test or identify other players who bet. According to Lombardi biographer David Maraniss, he told Rozelle, "I'll be honest with you. You know I did bet. I admit it. That's the farthest I'm going."

Rozelle indefinitely suspended Hornung and Detroit Lions defensive tackle Alex Karras, who also admitted to betting on games, on April 17, 1963. The commissioner also fined five other Lions $2,000 each for betting on the 1962 championship game and fined the Lions organization $2,000 for a lack of vigilance. Rozelle's swift action earned him praise as a strong and ethical commissioner, and his damage control was artful. He issued a statement that read:

> There is no evidence that any NFL player has given less than his best in playing any game. There is no evidence that any player has ever bet against his own team. There is no evidence that any NFL player has sold information to gamblers. There is clear evidence that some NFL players knowingly carried on undesirable associations which in some instances led to their betting on their own team to win and/or other National Football League games.

Hornung and Karras were reinstated for the 1964 season and resumed all-star careers.

Rozelle considered those suspensions his toughest decisions while in office. That same year, he made the decision he would regret most. He learned, along with the rest of America, on Friday, November 22, 1963, that President John F. Kennedy was assassinated in Dallas. Rozelle phoned White House press secretary Pierre Salinger and asked him if he thought NFL games should be played that weekend. Rozelle was inclined to play the games, and Salinger reinforced that stance. "It has been traditional in sports for athletes to perform in times of great personal tragedy," Rozelle said. "Football was Mr. Kennedy's game. He thrived on competition." Rozelle was harshly criticized as being disrespectful to the fallen president and was cast in an especially poor light when the AFL canceled its weekend games. Yet Rozelle's overall leadership earned him the designation as *Sports Illustrated*'s Sportsman of the Year for 1963.

He had no time to rest on his laurels, however. The pesky AFL was still in business, despite suffering several major defeats. Hunt conceded Dallas to the Cowboys and moved his Texans to Kansas City in 1963, renaming them the Chiefs. Barron Hilton could not compete with the Rams in Los Angeles, and after one season he moved the Chargers to San Diego. Boston owner Billy Sullivan was struggling to pay his bills. Harry Wismer's New York Titans, the AFL's pivotal franchise, went broke in 1962 and finished the season under league operation. But still the AFL would not go away. "To us, its endurance was mind-boggling," wrote former NFL executive Don Weiss.

The NFL was not as alarmed as it should have been when Sonny Werblin, a top entertainment agent, and four partners bought the AFL's New York franchise for $1 million on March 28, 1963. Werblin renamed the team the "Jets" and hired Head Coach Weeb Ewbank, who had guided the Colts to the 1958 and 1959 NFL championships. The older league also should have been more alarmed when Werblin negotiated the AFL's five-year, $36 million television contract with NBC, starting in 1965. "The NFL remained convinced that the upstart league was living on borrowed time," Weiss said. "And all it needed to do was keep fighting and await the inevitable."

Werblin's signing of Alabama quarterback Joe Namath to a three-year, $427,000 contract on January 2, 1965, would force the NFL to reconsider its confident position. Yet this historic development was as accidental as it was consequential. Despite new ownership, the Jets had losing records in both 1963 and 1964. Werblin applied his show business principles to pro football and told Ewbank they needed a star-quality quarterback. Werblin was referring to Jerry Rhome from Tulsa. The Jets took him in the 1964 draft, when he had a year of college eligibility left, and brought him to New York before the 1965 draft to offer him a contract. "What happened next was a faux pas that may have changed the course of professional football," wrote Chuck Knox, then the Jets' offensive line coach, in his autobiography. Knox revealed that Werblin soured on Rhome because he jumped into the back seat of a limousine without waiting for Werblin's wife. "I don't believe this!" Werblin said. "This is not star quality."

Knox could not have been more pleased. He had been lobbying Ewbank to draft Namath, despite his serious knee injuries at Alabama. Knox had respected the player's talent ever since Namath was a junior high school basketball player in western Pennsylvania and Knox was a rival coach. Before the 1965 draft, which was held November 28, 1964, the Jets traded their rights to Rhome to the Houston Oilers for a first-round pick, which the Jets used to select Namath. The Jets had little trouble outbidding the Cardinals, who picked Namath in the first round of the NFL draft, and signed him a day after he was named MVP of a 21–17 loss to Texas in the Orange Bowl. Namath's signing raised the AFL's credibility to new heights. It also sent a message to the NFL that the war between the leagues was a long way from over.

Both leagues spent as much as $25 million to sign rookies in 1965, and veterans were quick to demand higher salaries. "If Joe Namath is worth four-hundred thousand dollars, then I'm worth a million dollars," said quarterback Frank Ryan, who had led the Browns to the 1964 NFL championship. NFL owners started to wonder if the price of victory over the AFL was becoming too high.

Buffalo Bills owner Ralph Wilson said in *Going Long*,

After the Namath contract in early sixty-five, merger stuff started behind the scenes. Sonny Werblin and I were appointed to talk to Carroll Rosenbloom. Sonny was against it and never came to the meeting. Carroll had a little cottage on the beach in South Florida, and we discussed a merger. There was such hostility between the leagues that you couldn't merge and just start playing each other.

Rosenbloom suggested the leagues could hold a common draft and inter-league exhibition games for four years and then realign into one league as animosity receded. Wilson recalled meeting with Rosenbloom seven or eight times to set the stage for a merger. Wilson said,

> One time I met with him and Pete Rozelle and Tex Schramm. The NFL wanted money to let us in. I said, "How much?" They said, "Fifty million." I said, "Forget it." We began to work things out, and I told Sonny, "This sounds great." He said, "No, I want to fight." And so did Wayne Valley in Oakland. But the rest of us in smaller cities thought this was our salvation. In the long run, the NFL would put us out of business because they had the big cities. They were going to get much more television money.

Werblin was not the only one who still wanted to fight. "I hated 'em," Schramm said many years later. "There are days when I still hate 'em."

Rozelle also wanted to keep fighting, for the war had become personal for him. "Having endured more than six years of acrimony, nasty accusations, and legal challenges, Rozelle certainly was reluctant to abandon this struggle," Weiss wrote. "A competitor in his own right, Pete liked a good fight and in many respects had come to relish this one, while growing even more confident that the NFL was about to win it."

By early 1966, however, financial considerations tempered even Schramm's combativeness. He was jolted by the high cost of signing players in the 1965 draft and was jolted again in the 1966 draft, held November 27, 1965. That the NFL was signing most of its 1966 picks brought him little consolation. The NFL signed 75 percent of its 232 draft choices, and the AFL signed 46 percent of its 181 picks. Of the 111 players both leagues drafted, seventy-nine signed with NFL teams, twenty-eight with AFL teams, and four went unsigned. But the NFL could not consider itself a big winner, especially not at the prices it was paying.

Before the 1966 draft, the Cowboys set their sights on Illinois fullback Jim Grabowski. "We always signed who we wanted to sign," Schramm recalled.

> Since he was one of the first players to start using an agent, we knew it would cost a lot of money to sign him. We tried to sign him but failed, so we didn't draft him. Green Bay wanted him, too. The Packers had a lot of money in those days. So we were a little afraid and pulled back and picked [guard] John Niland instead. The Packers, of course, got Grabowski. I could see something developing in which the teams with money were going to get better, and the others would fall off. Once you take away the competitive aspect of the game, you destroy the package.

Schramm concluded in February 1966 that it was time to explore a merger. He ran a few proposals by Reeves, his former boss, and received encouragement. Schramm then told Rozelle that he wanted to discreetly open merger talks with Hunt. Rozelle approved, as long as Schramm would keep him updated on the discussions. Schramm's approach was to negotiate in good faith, but he favored an all-out war if he was rebuffed.

That same month, Foss gave a speech hinting that he considered the war between the leagues, and his days as commissioner, near an end. Speaking to the Lynchburg Sports Club in Virginia, Foss predicted the leagues were about to merge under one commissioner. "All the club owners in both leagues are practical businessmen, and they'll force a championship playoff, no matter what any commissioner thinks," Foss said. "I've said for years that the two leagues would play some day and it now appears the playoff will take place in 1967 or at the end of the 1966 season."

Foss already was cleaning out his desk and resigned April 7, 1966, at a league meeting in Houston. Owners too often found him unavailable and questioned the amount of time he was devoting to the AFL, especially when he went hunting in Africa as host of ABC's new outdoors series, *The American Sportsman*.

Hunt reflected,

> Joe Foss brought major prestige to the league in a sense that few people could. His name really meant something nationwide when the name "American Football League" didn't mean anything. Joe was a battler. He had done a good job in the early years, but I think he felt the time was there for a change. We felt we needed more of a hands-on person.

Raiders coach and general manager Al Davis replaced Foss. While owners discussed candidates, Oilers owner Bud Adams said, "What we need is some ruthless bastard who won't have any compunction about taking the war right to them." Valley said he had just the man. "Take my genius!" he shouted. One of Davis's first acts as commissioner was to break up a fight between Adams and Houston sports columnist Jack Gallagher. Davis was bent on starting fights, however, not stopping them.

He probably would not have accepted the job had he known that merger talks had just started. Hunt was about to fly from Kansas City to Houston for the April meeting when Schramm phoned and asked to meet about an important matter. Hunt said he could stop off in Dallas, and they could talk at the airport. "We met at the statue of the Texas Ranger inside Love Field that evening and went out to his car in the parking lot," Hunt recalled. "There was just a feeling that there would be a little more privacy if we did that. [But] it looked very suspicious to have two guys out there in the parking lot."

Schramm made his pitch for a merger, but he wanted the Raiders and Jets relocated from NFL markets and Rozelle to oversee both leagues. Schramm not only had to win over Hunt but some of the NFL owners, too. Giants owner Wellington Mara and 49ers president Lou Spadia were skeptical about a merger unless they could get guarantees that their crosstown rivals would move. Yet they gave Schramm the impression neither would undermine a merger. Schramm told Hunt on May 3 that he expected each of the nine AFL teams to pay $2 million to join the NFL.

A week later, Hunt told Schramm he was confident they could make a deal. Schramm delivered an optimistic update to Rozelle, who suggested that they meet with Mara and Spadia in New York before the owners' mid-May meeting in Washington, D.C. Mara and Spadia seemed to have cooled toward a merger, however. Schramm and Rozelle then decided it would be premature to discuss the proposal at the owners' meeting. Instead, they decided to approach the owners discreetly and quietly build a consensus.

When the owners met in Washington, Schramm was in for a shock. Mara nearly blew any possibility of a merger when he announced the signing of former Bills place kicker Pete Gogolak. This move did not technically violate Foss and Rozelle's no-tampering pact because Gogolak had played out his option and was a free agent. But he was the first notable player to switch leagues, and Davis felt justified to retaliate by going after unsigned NFL stars. Rozelle approved the Gogolak signing because, he said, it did not violate league rules. NFL owners could only hold their ears and wait for the explosion.

As Weiss, an assistant to NFL public relations director Jim Kensil, described it,

> Most alarming of all was what the signing revealed about Rozelle's attitude toward the AFL. Conciliation was not on his agenda. Reactions among owners were tremendous and volatile. Sitting in the room with them, I still can remember how astonished I was by the outrage being expressed. Jim Kensil and I had been alerted by Rozelle that Mara was going to make his announcement, but I couldn't have anticipated

the storm that erupted. Schisms among owners were apparent. Exchanges between old friends, such as Mara and Vince Lombardi, who was representing Green Bay, were particularly heated. Lombardi was so furious that his face turned red. It really hit the fan. Amid these exchanges, the possibility of a merger became exposed—and so did hints of Rozelle's opposition to it!

Schramm, now realizing the depth of Rozelle's opposition to a merger, quickly convened a meeting of key owners and executives to save his negotiations with Hunt. He met with Mara, Spadia, Lombardi, Rosenbloom, the Cleveland Browns' Art Modell, and Cardinals co-owner Stormy Bidwill. All wanted to end the signing war and asked Schramm to tell Rozelle they were prepared to pursue the merger on their own. Schramm went to Rozelle's suite and said, "It was decided that if you're not going to lead us in the merger, then we're going to go ahead without you."

Rozelle was furious and conflicted, but he finally agreed. "All right, let's go," he said.

After they left Washington, Rozelle and several owners met in New York to reach a consensus on a merger proposal. He then flew to Dallas, where he and Schramm prepared an offer to Hunt. Davis, meanwhile, was asking AFL teams to make huge salary offers to NFL stars whose contracts were up for renewal. Hunt could not stop Davis without revealing the merger negotiations or letting Davis know he would be out of a job. Among the NFL stars persuaded to switch leagues were Bears tight end Mike Ditka, Rams quarterback Roman Gabriel, and 49ers quarterback John Brodie.

Schramm warned Hunt this raiding might inflame NFL owners and prompt them to abandon the merger. He told Hunt that all fifteen NFL owners agreed to the proposal crafted in New York but that it could unravel if the AFL demanded too many changes. Hunt met in New York with his owners, who initially resisted paying the NFL $18 million or relocating the Raiders and Jets. On June 5, Hunt and Schramm reached an agreement in principle. On June 7, Rozelle received approval from his owners. Davis did not learn of the merger until that night, and Rozelle announced the historic deal the next day.

Rozelle became the sole commissioner. No franchises would move. A common draft and inter-league exhibition play would start in 1967, with a single NFL schedule set for 1970. Each league would add a franchise in 1968, with the franchise fees going to the fifteen NFL owners. AFL teams would pay the NFL $18 million over twenty years, with the cash compensating the Giants and 49ers for sharing their territories.

The merger could not go through, however, until the leagues were certain it complied with antitrust laws. Rozelle sought support from New York congressman Emanuel Celler, chairman of the House Judiciary Committee. Celler vehemently opposed the merger, however, and by mid-October it appeared a lost cause. The merger was rescued by House majority leader Hale Boggs of Louisiana, who was told through an intermediary that passing a merger bill would all but guarantee an NFL franchise for New Orleans. Boggs attached the NFL's antitrust relief to an anti-inflation bill that President Lyndon Johnson viewed as a priority. According to the *New York Times*, Rozelle and Boggs met October 21, an hour before the vote on the crucial bill.

"Just for the record, I assume we can say the franchise for New Orleans is firm?" Boggs asked. When Rozelle replied that New Orleans' chances for a team looked good but that he could not make any promises before checking with his owners, Boggs said, "Well, Pete, why don't you go back and check with the owners? I'll hold things up here until you get back."

Boggs had forced Rozelle's hand. The commissioner said, "That's all right, Hale. You can count on their approval." Eleven days later, New Orleans became the first expansion franchise in the post-merger NFL.

Once the merger was under way, Rozelle suggested each league appoint three owners to serve on a joint planning committee. Setting a championship game after the 1966 season was first on the agenda. "The two championship teams the year before had been Buffalo and Green Bay," Hunt recalled. "Nobody could envision wanting to play in Buffalo or Green Bay in January, so we explored the idea of playing at a neutral site. That was very revolutionary at the time."

Los Angeles was appealing because of its large stadiums and warm weather. Rozelle wanted to play the first championship game at the Rose Bowl in suburban Pasadena, but stadium officials feared the NFL would steal thunder from the annual Rose Bowl Classic on New Year's Day. The merger committee opted for the Los Angeles Memorial Coliseum, a downtown stadium that could seat 100,000 people. Hunt named the game the Super Bowl, after a high-bouncing SuperBall that entertained his three children. The first Super Bowl officially was called "World Championship Game AFL vs. NFL." It matched the Chiefs and the Packers on January 15 and drew a crowd of 61,946, well short of a sellout. But this championship game's future obviously was promising. About 60 million viewers tuned in to NBC or CBS, which charged $75,000 and $85,000, respectively, for one-minute commercials.

Hunt, who was inspired to put his money and energy into pro football after watching the Colts beat the Giants in the 1958 title game, now owned a team playing for even higher stakes. His Chiefs lost 35-10 to Lombardi's Packers and was reminded after the loss that acceptance from the older league would come only grudgingly. When reporters prodded him to compare the leagues, Lombardi replied, "I don't think Kansas City compares with the best teams in the NFL. Dallas is a better team. There. That's what you wanted me to say, isn't it?"

Hunt got his payback three years later in a 23–7 Super Bowl victory over the Minnesota Vikings in New Orleans. But the moment that really made the Foolish Club seem smart arrived January 12, 1969. The Jets, a seventeen-and-one-half-point underdog, upset the Colts 16–7 and vindicated Namath's pregame guarantee of a Jets' victory. Ewbank became the first coach ever to win a Super Bowl and both NFL and AFL championships.

NBC announcer Curt Gowdy said in the game's closing minutes, "Ladies and gentlemen, you're sitting in on one of the most amazing upsets in the history of sports. This game may also change the future of football. If the AFL wins, the fans probably will accept them, embrace them, and there will be a lot of things changed in pro football."

Pro football, in truth, already was radically transformed. Ameche's 1958 run had been a harbinger of change—for the next thirteen months and for the next fifty years.

Bibliography

Associated Press. "Rozelle, Foss Think Two Leagues Can Live Together Harmoniously." *Washington Post,* February 9, 1960.

Bell, Upton. "A Private Man in a Public Place." *Boston Globe,* June 19, 1983.

Bengtson, Phil, and Todd Hunt. *Packer Dynasty.* Garden City, NY: Doubleday & Co., Inc., 1969.

Bisher, Furman. "Billy Cannon and the Pro Football War." *Sport Magazine,* June 1960.

Brokaw, Tom. *The Greatest Generation.* New York: Random House, 1998.

Callahan, Tom. *Johnny U: The Life and Times of John Unitas.* New York: Crown Publishing, 2006.

Covitz, Randy. "This Pick Was a Dandy." *Kansas City Star,* April 13, 2000.

Daly, Dan, and Bob O'Donnell. *The Pro Football Chronicle: The Complete (Well Almost) Record of the Best Players, the Greatest Passes, the Hardest Hits, the Biggest Scandals & the Funniest Stories in Pro Football.* New York: Collier Books, 1990.

Day, Chuck, and Don Weiss. *The Making of the Super Bowl: The Inside Story of the World's Greatest Sporting Event.* New York: Contemporary Books, 2003.

Dent, Jim. *King of the Cowboys: The Life and Times of Jerry Jones.* Holbrook, MA: Adams, 1995.

DeVito, Carlo. *Wellington: The Maras, the Giants, and the City of New York.* Chicago: Triumph Books, 2006.

Dienhart, Tom, Joe Hoppel, and Dave Sloan, eds. *The Sporting News Complete Super Bowl Book.* St. Louis: The Sporting News Publishing, 1994.

Eldridge, Larry, Jr. "The Turning Point." *Super Bowl XVIII Program,* January 22, 1984.

Florence, Mal. "Cannon's Houston Contract Signed Before Sugar Bowl." *Los Angeles Times,* April 28, 1960.

Fortunato, John A. *Commissioner: The Legacy of Pete Rozelle.* Lanham, MD: Taylor Trade Publishing, 2006.

Foss, Joe, and Donna Wild Foss. *A Proud American: The Autobiography of Joe Foss.* New York: Pocket Books, 1992.

Gruver, Ed. *The American Football League: A Year-by-Year History, 1960–1969.* Jefferson, NC: McFarland & Co., Inc., 1997.

Gunther, Marc, and Bill Carter. *Monday Night Mayhem: The Inside Story of ABC's Monday Night Football.* New York: William Morrow, 1988.

Halas, George S. *Halas: An Autobiography.* With Gwen Morgan and Arthur Veysey. Chicago: Bonus Books, 1986.

Halberstam, David. *The Fifties.* New York: Ballantine Books, 1993.

———. *Summer of '49,* New York: William Morrow & Co., 1989.

Harris, David. *The League: The Rise and Decline of the NFL.* New York: Bantam Books, 1986.

Hornung, Paul, and Billy Reed. *Lombardi and Me: Players, Coaches, and Colleagues Talk About the Man and the Myth.* Chicago: Triumph Books, 2006.

Knox, Chuck, and Bill Plaschke. *Hard Knox: The Life of an NFL Coach.* New York: Harcourt Brace Jovanovich, 1988.

Longman, Jere. "Never Forgotten, Billy Cannon Is Now Forgiven." *New York Times,* December 28, 2003.

MacCambridge, Michael. *America's Game: The Epic Story of How Pro Football Captured A Nation.* New York: Random House, 2004.

Mann, Jack. "The Best Football Game Ever Played." *Boston Globe,* September 29, 1974.

Maraniss, David. *When Pride Still Mattered: A Life of Vince Lombardi.* New York: Simon & Schuster, 1999.

Maule, Tex. "The Best Football Game Ever Played." *Sports Illustrated,* January 5, 1959.

———. "The Infighting Was Vicious." *Sports Illustrated,* February 8, 1960.

McKee, Sandra. "Turning 40, Game Still Has Great Hold." *Baltimore Sun,* December 27, 1998.

Miller, Jeff. *Going Long: The Wild 10-Year Saga of the Renegade American Football League in the Words of Those Who Lived It.* New York: McGraw-Hill, 1995.

Moore, David. "Building America's Team." *Dallas Morning News,* February 13, 2000.

Oates, Bob. "Rams Lose Cannon." *Los Angeles Examiner,* June 21, 1960.

O'Brien, Michael. *Vince: A Personal Biography of Vince Lombardi.* New York: Morrow, 1987.

Powers, Ron. *Super Tube: The Rise of Television Sports.* New York: Coward-McCann, Inc., 1984.

Steadman, John. "Colts-Giants II: Greatest Letdown." *Baltimore Sun,* December 26, 1999.

———. "December 28, 1958." *Inside Sports,* January 1989.

St. John, Bob. *Tex! The Man Who Built the Dallas Cowboys.* Englewood Cliffs, NJ: Prentice Hall, 1988.

Stoltz, Jeremy. "The West Coast Offense." chi.scout.com, May 3, 2007.

Stram, Hank. *They're Playing My Game.* With Lou Sahadi. Chicago: Triumph Books, 2006.

Taylor, Otis. *The Need to Win.* With Mark Stallard. Champaign, IL: Sports Publishing, 2003.

Terzian, Jim. *New York Giants.* New York: Macmillan, 1973.

Time.com. "A Man's Game." *Time,* November 30, 1959.

United Press International. "Foss: Merger Was Blunder." *Milwaukee Sentinel,* January 25, 1967.

Zimmer, Jon, Randall Liu, and Matt Marini, eds. *Official 2007 NFL Record & Fact Book.* New York: National Football League Books, 2007.

Zimmerman, Paul. *The New Thinking Man's Guide to Pro Football.* New York: Simon & Schuster, 1984.

———. "When Sid Was Caesar." *Sports Illustrated,* February 1, 1988.

Index

About the Author

Jonathan Rand is a longtime sports reporter, columnist, and author with a special interest in professional football and its history. His previous books include *Run It! And Let's Get the Hell Out of Here! The 100 Best Plays in Pro Football History; 300 Pounds of Attitude: The Wildest Stories and Craziest Characters the NFL Has Ever Seen; Fields of Honor: The Pat Tillman Story; The Gridiron's Greatest Quarterbacks;* and *The Gridiron's Greatest Linebackers.*

Rand has worked on the sports staffs of the *Kansas City Star, Miami Herald,* and *Miami News* and covered every major professional, college, and Olympic event. While at the *Star,* he wrote an award-winning daily column for fifteen years and also covered the Chiefs and the NFL at large. His assignments in Miami included covering the Miami Dolphins during their perfect 1972 season. Rand has covered hundreds of NFL games, including twenty-three Super Bowls.

In addition to his book projects, Rand currently is a columnist for kcchiefs.com, the official website of the Kansas City Chiefs. A native of New York City, he has lived in Kansas City, Missouri, since 1979.